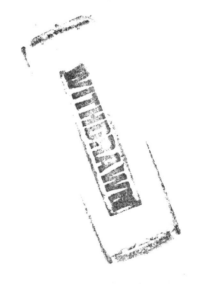

SRI SATYA
SAI BABA

SPIRITUAL LEADERS AND THINKERS

JOHN CALVIN

DALAI LAMA (TENZIN GYATSO)

MARY BAKER EDDY

JONATHAN EDWARDS

DESIDERIUS ERASMUS

MOHANDAS GANDHI

AYATOLLAH RUHOLLAH KHOMEINI

MARTIN LUTHER

AIMEE SEMPLE McPHERSON

THOMAS MERTON

SRI SATYA SAI BABA

ELISABETH SCHÜSSLER FIORENZA

EMANUEL SWEDENBORG

SPIRITUAL
LEADERS AND
THINKERS

SRI SATYA SAI BABA

Masoud Kheirabadi
Portland State University

Introductory Essay by
Martin E. Marty, Professor Emeritus
University of Chicago Divinity School

CHELSEA HOUSE
PUBLISHERS
A Haights Cross Communications Company ®
Philadelphia

COVER: Sri Satya Sai Baba waves to his followers.

CHELSEA HOUSE PUBLISHERS

VP, New Product Development Sally Cheney
Director of Production Kim Shinners
Creative Manager Takeshi Takahashi
Manufacturing Manager Diann Grasse

Staff for SRI SATYA SAI BABA

Executive Editor Lee Marcott
Editorial Assistant Carla Greenberg
Production Editor Noelle Nardone
Photo Editor Sarah Bloom
Series and Cover Designer Keith Trego
Layout 21st Century Publishing and Communications, Inc.

A Haights Cross Communications ◥ Company ®

www.chelseahouse.com

First Printing

9 8 7 6 5 4 3 2 1

Library of Congress Cataloging-in-Publication Data

Kheirabadi, Masoud, 1951–
    Sri Satya Sai Baba / Masoud Kheirabadi.
        p. cm.—(Spiritual leaders and thinkers)
        Includes bibliographical references and index.
ISBN 0-7910-8104-4 (hardcover)
    1. Sathya Sai Baba, 1926- 2. Gurus—India—Biography. I. Title. II. Series.
BL1175.S385K54 2005
294.5'092—dc22

                                                            2005002727

CONTENTS

Foreword

Why become acquainted with notable people when making efforts to understand the religions of the world?

Most of the faith communities number hundreds of millions of people. What can attention paid to one tell about more, if not most, to say nothing of *all*, their adherents? Here is why:

The people in this series are exemplars. If you permit me to take a little detour through medieval dictionaries, their role will become clear.

In medieval lexicons, the word *exemplum* regularly showed up with a peculiar definition. No one needs to know Latin to see that it relates to "example" and "exemplary." But back then, *exemplum* could mean something very special.

That "ex-" at the beginning of such words signals "taking out" or "cutting out" something or other. Think of to "excise" something, which is to snip it out. So, in the more interesting dictionaries, an *exemplum* was referred to as "a clearing in the woods," something cut out of the forests.

These religious figures are *exempla*, figurative clearings in the woods of life. These clearings and these people perform three functions:

First, they define. You can be lost in the darkness, walking under the leafy canopy, above the undergrowth, plotless in the pathless forest. Then you come to a clearing. It defines with a sharp line: there, the woods end; here, the open space begins.

Great religious figures are often stumblers in the dark woods.

We see them emerging in the bright light of the clearing, blinking, admitting that they had often been lost in the mysteries of existence, tangled up with the questions that plague us all, wandering without definition. Then they discover the clearing, and, having done so, they point our way to it. We then learn more of who we are and where we are. Then we can set our own direction.

Second, the *exemplum*, the clearing in the woods of life, makes possible a brighter vision. Great religious pioneers in every case experience illumination and then they reflect their light into the hearts and minds of others. In Buddhism, a key word is *enlightenment.* In the Bible, "the people who walked in darkness have seen a great light." They see it because their prophets or savior brought them to the sun in the clearing.

Finally, when you picture a clearing in the woods, an *exemplum*, you are likely to see it as a place of cultivation. Whether in the Black Forest of Germany, on the American frontier, or in the rain forests of Brazil, the clearing is the place where, with light and civilization, residents can cultivate, can produce culture. As an American moviegoer, my mind's eye remembers cinematic scenes of frontier days and places that pioneers hacked out of the woods. There, they removed stones, planted, built a cabin, made love and produced families, smoked their meat, hung out laundered clothes, and read books. All that can happen in clearings.

In the case of these religious figures, planting and cultivating and harvesting are tasks in which they set an example and then inspire or ask us to follow. Most of us would not have the faintest idea how to find or be found by God, to nurture the Holy Spirit, to create a philosophy of life without guidance. It is not likely that most of us would be satisfied with our search if we only consulted books of dogma or philosophy, though such may come to have their place in the clearing.

Philosopher Søren Kierkegaard properly pointed out that you cannot learn to swim by being suspended from the ceiling on a belt and reading a "How To" book on swimming. You learn because a parent or an instructor plunges you into water, supports you when necessary, teaches you breathing and motion, and then releases you to swim on your own.

Kierkegaard was not criticizing the use of books. I certainly have nothing against books. If I did, I would not be commending this series to you, as I am doing here. For guidance and courage in the spiritual quest, or—and this is by no means unimportant!—in intellectual pursuits, involving efforts to understand the paths others have taken, there seems to be no better way than to follow a fellow mortal, but a man or woman of genius, depth, and daring. We "see" them through books like these.

Exemplars come in very different styles and forms. They bring differing kinds of illumination, and then suggest or describe diverse patterns of action to those who join them. In the case of the present series, it is possible for someone to repudiate or disagree with *all* the religious leaders in this series. It is possible also to be nonreligious and antireligious and therefore to disregard the truth claims of all of them. It is more difficult, however, to ignore them. Atheists, agnostics, adherents, believers, and fanatics alike live in cultures that are different for the presence of these people. "Leaders and thinkers" they may be, but most of us do best to appraise their thought in the context of the lives they lead or have led.

If it is possible to reject them all, it is impossible to affirm everything that all of them were about. They disagree with each other, often in basic ways. Sometimes they develop their positions and ways of thinking by separating themselves from all the others. If they met each other, they would likely judge each other cruelly. Yet the lives of each and all of them make a contribution to the intellectual and spiritual quests of those who go in ways other than theirs. There are tens of thousands of religions in the world, and millions of faith communities. Every one of them has been shaped by founders and interpreters, agents of change and prophets of doom or promise. It may seem arbitrary to walk down a bookshelf and let a finger fall on one or another, almost accidentally. This series may certainly look arbitrary in this way. Why precisely the choice of these exemplars?

In some cases, it is clear that the publishers have chosen someone who has a constituency. Many of the world's 54 million Lutherans may be curious about where they got their name, who the man Martin Luther was. Others are members of a community but choose isolation: The hermit monk Thomas Merton is typical. Still others are exiled and achieve their work far from the clearing in which they grew up; here the Dalai Lama is representative. Quite a number of the selected leaders had been made unwelcome, or felt unwelcome in the clearings, in their own childhoods and youth. This reality has almost always been the case with women like Mary Baker Eddy or Aimee Semple McPherson. Some are extremely controversial: Ayatollah Ruhollah Khomeini stands out. Yet to read of this life and thought as one can in this series will be illuminating in much of the world of conflict today.

Reading of religious leaders can be a defensive act: Study the lives of certain ones among them and you can ward off spiritual—and sometimes even militant—assaults by people who follow them. Reading and learning can be a personally positive act: Most of these figures led lives that we can indeed call exemplary. Such lives can throw light on communities of people who are in no way tempted to follow them. I am not likely to be drawn to the hermit life, will not give up my allegiance to medical doctors, or be successfully nonviolent. Yet Thomas Merton reaches me and many non-Catholics in our communities; Mary Baker Eddy reminds others that there are more ways than one to approach healing; Mohandas Gandhi stings the conscience of people in cultures like ours where resorting to violence is too frequent, too easy.

Finally, reading these lives tells something about how history is made by imperfect beings. None of these subjects is a god, though some of them claimed that they had special access to the divine, or that they were like windows that provided for illumination to that which is eternal. Most of their stories began with inauspicious childhoods. Sometimes they were victimized, by parents or by leaders of religions from which they later broke.

Some of them were unpleasant and abrasive. They could be ungracious toward those who were near them and impatient with laggards. If their lives were symbolic clearings, places for light, many of them also knew clouds and shadows and the fall of night. How they met the challenges of life and led others to face them is central to the plot of all of them.

I have often used a rather unexciting concept to describe what I look for in books: *interestingness*. The authors of these books, one might say, had it easy, because the characters they treat are themselves so interesting. But the authors also had to be interesting and responsible. If, as they wrote, they would have dulled the personalities of their bright characters, that would have been a flaw as marring as if they had treated their subjects without combining fairness and criticism, affection and distance. To my eye, and I hope in yours, they take us to spiritual and intellectual clearings that are so needed in our dark times.

Martin E. Marty
The University of Chicago

Author's Note

The events surrounding the life of Satya Sai Baba are so shrouded in myth, folklore, and pious fabrication by his devotees that differentiating truth from imagination has become almost an impossible task. Most available accounts of his life rely heavily on Sai Baba's primary biographer, N. Kasturi, who has compiled the historical details of his life in a lengthy multivolume book. Likewise, I have largely relied on Kasturi while writing the biographical chapters of this book, especially chapters covering Sai Baba's life from birth to Godhood. The Internet also provides a wealth of information on Sai Baba's life, character, deeds, and discourses. I have mainly utilized the sites that cover his discourses.

Another note that I need to make is that like many other illustrious global celebrities, Sai Baba has some critics, who have doubted the integrity of his character and work. Controversies about his misdeeds, ranging from his being a petty magician to a sex abuser, abound. For the purposes of this book, I have tried not to dwell upon controversies but rather to focus on positive aspects of his life, including his intellectual discourses and humanitarian activities.

I am indebted to several individuals who have assisted me in my writing. I am thankful to Mozhgan Ilanloo, and to Dr. Nahid Sajjadian for helping with the initial research. I am also heavily

indebted to my friend Daniel O'Donnell, for his invaluable contributions to both the research and the writing; without his help,
this book would not have been finished on time for publication.

Masoud Kheirabadi
December 14, 2004
Portland, Oregon

1

Appointment with a Living God

There is only one religion, the religion of Love;
There is only one language, the language of the Heart;
There is only one caste, the caste of Humanity;
There is only one law, the law of Karma;
There is only one God, He is Omnipresent.

—Satya Sai Baba

S arah has come all the way from her home in London to see the legendary Bhagavan Sri Satya Sai Baba in his birthplace, the small town of Puttaparthi in southern India.[1] Although she is physically exhausted from her long trip, she cannot sleep. Her mind spins excitedly with endless thoughts, secret hopes, and unanswered questions. Tomorrow, she is about to meet a man whom everybody talks about; a man who, according to his followers, is the greatest living *avatar* ("embodiment of the divine") on Earth, the true incarnation of God and the most celebrated mystic of the modern age. A Man-God who claims to be able to conduct miracles, materialize objects, cure the diseased, and even resurrect the dead!

Although her spirit is flying high, Sarah feels a bit anxious about tomorrow's meeting. As an educated woman, she has read the works of many of the world's well-known prophets and mystics, but she has never actually come face to face with any major spiritual figure. In the twenty-first century, when experimental science has advanced to such a degree that humankind is on the verge of recreating its own through artificial cloning, she is about to visit a man whose claims of divinity—if true—should allow him to create and recreate at will and without the help of science. She has traveled all this way to see with her own eyes a man who claims to be omniscient, omnipotent, and omnipresent. His extraordinary claims seem impossible, and Sarah cannot help but wonder—could they be true? Is Sai Baba who he claims to be? Is he a living God?

Sarah has read or heard about many of the amazing miracles and supernatural powers attributed to Sai Baba, but what attracts her to him more than anything else is his message of universal love and tolerance. In a world torn by excessive greed, blind fanaticism, ethnic conflict, devastating wars, and global terrorism, Baba's message of love, peace, unity, and devotion to an all-embracing God sounds refreshing to her ears. Sincerely believing in love's power to overcome hatred, deception, violence, and cruelty, characteristics currently tearing the world apart, Sarah admires those who champion love.

She remembers reading about Baba's message of love—how he has come to light the lamp of love in all people's hearts and to see it shine, day by day, with added luster. Sarah likes the fact that he does not associate himself or his message with any exclusive religion, nor does he deny the rights or authenticity of other religions. He does not advertise any particular religious sect, creed, or cause, but advocates an all-inclusive faith with spiritual teachings based on love and harmony among all humankind. According to his followers, Sai Baba is the true manifestation of unconditional love. His major spiritual principle is love—the path of love, the virtue of love, the duty of love, and the obligation of love. Love, according to Baba, is the only true remedy for human loneliness, emptiness, and fear.

Sarah is very tired. It has taken her more than 16 hours to travel by train from Bombay to Puttaparthi. Her body still aches after sitting for hours on the hard wooden seats in the old, overcrowded train. From the train, she witnesses the extreme poverty in the streets of Bombay, and the lofty, selfless spirit of the Indian poor surprises her. She remembers how her fellow Indian travelers, who were sitting next to and across from her throughout her trip, constantly and kindly entertained her by playing music and singing spiritual songs inspired by a book of prayers to Ramakrishna.

Sarah finds India to be an amazing country, a country that her favorite British anthropologist Michael Wood referred to as "The Empire of Spirit"; a land with a long and very rich spiritual history.[2] It is the birthplace of two of the world's major religions, Hinduism and Buddhism, and it has also introduced the world to many other spiritual faiths, such as Jainism and Sikhism. As she finally falls asleep, Sarah is certain that only a country like India could become the birthplace of so many spiritual faiths and so many avatars, such as Sai Baba, whom she will finally meet tomorrow.

The next day, as early as 3:00 A.M., thousands of visitors, who, like Sarah, have come to see Sai Baba, begin walking in large groups toward the southern part of the ashram, where Baba's house is located. The majority of the people are dressed in white attire, with women wearing loose Indian-style saris and men in long, loose, Punjabi-style apparel. Sarah, who could hardly sleep the night before, wakes up after just a few hours and is soon on her way to see the man whom she has traveled such a long way to meet, despite many hardships. She rushes to catch up with the crowd, joining a group of people chanting spiritual songs as they walk toward Baba's house. The sheer number of people in the crowd, as well as their racial and ethnic diversity, amaze Sarah. There are both men and women, from all walks of life, with different skin colors, and from different ethnic backgrounds, socioeconomic classes, and age groups.

Minutes later, Sarah is walking shoulder to shoulder with a young Japanese couple who are extremely excited to see Baba. She begins a conversation with this married couple and discovers that they are both devoted followers of Sai Baba. The husband refers to Baba as the creator who deserves worship. Intrigued by his statement, she listens as the man begins to explain how Baba is the true incarnation of the almighty God—the very creator of the universe. Baba deserves to be worshiped, he continues, by all human beings that believe in God, because Baba is the absolute God. He then talks about how knowing Baba has brought him the long-awaited peace he once desperately searched for, and how believing in Baba has completely and positively transformed his life. The true believers of Baba, he adds, will overcome their soul's emptiness and their mind's turbulence, eventually reaching ultimate peace and tranquility in their own lives and in their relations with others.

Though Sarah has long appreciated Sai Baba's love for humanity, while finding his compassion for world peace and unity admirable, she, nevertheless, has not been able to accept Baba as her God, her creator who deserves worship. Like many of her fellow country people, she has grown up as a Christian, believing in one almighty, unseen God who does not represent himself in human form—Jesus being an exception. She, like many followers of other monotheistic religions, also does not believe in reincarnation, so accepting God's appearance in the form of a man goes against her principal religious beliefs.

As the crowd nears a large meeting hall, which looks a lot like a covered stadium, uniformed guards begin sorting the visitors into two separate groups, with men in one group and women in the other. They are told to wait outside the hall's entrance doors until the guards signal the appropriate time to enter the building. There are many people waiting to get into the hall. Official attendants organize the crowd into smaller groups, with each group containing about 50 people. Several female guards walk around and in a commanding tone order the women to stay in their assigned spaces. As Sarah looks around, she estimates that there are about 60 to 70 groups of women waiting in their assigned spaces to enter the hall. After standing for a while, she, like many members of her group, sits down on the ground and waits.

As she waits, a cool breeze caresses Sarah's long blond hair. Birds sing sweetly in the tall trees of the ashram. Sarah cannot remember the last time she was awake this early in the morning. Swallowing the fresh, clear, cool autumn air in the charming rural atmosphere of Puttaparthi rejuvenates her spirit. Moments likes these are very rare when living in a polluted crowded city like London. Resting her head on her knee, Sarah's thoughts return to Sai Baba. She tries to imagine what it will be like when she finally sees Baba, the man who the young Japanese follower confidently referred to as the creator of the universe. She secretly wishes that meeting Baba will cultivate the seeds of love in the fertile ground of her soul. She wants to be able to love unconditionally, to love for the sake of love and not because of her own selfish desire. She has no doubt that if she opens her heart to true unconditional love, she will be able to achieve genuine peace and tranquility in her life.

A mysterious-sounding bell breaks her train of thought. People quickly rise and are guided toward the hall. As Sarah stands, she finds that her knees are sore; she has been sitting for about three hours, waiting to see Sai Baba. The female guards direct the women toward a small entrance door assigned specifically to female visitors. At the entrance, three female guards carefully search all those who enter the hall. After passing through the entrance door, women are organized again into new groups and ordered to sit and wait.

A large red carpet in the middle of the hall separates the men from the women. Altogether, there are several thousand people sitting. Waiting. Hoping. Praying. What is it that brings so many people from so many different parts of the world here? Sarah quietly thinks. Coming from so many different religious and ethnic backgrounds, what do all these people have in common? Many white people from rich, technologically advanced countries seem to be just as excited to see Baba as those people from poor, lesser-developed nations. As female guards warn women against mixing with the men on the other side, Sarah wonders why is it necessary to segregate the women from the men. Is it because Sai Baba and his employees want them to better concentrate on their spiritual journey rather than being distracted by unnecessary thoughts?

Suddenly, strange music fills the hall. Almost every person in the hall turns his or her face curiously toward one side of the hall; a lot of whispering seems to be coming from that area. Something is happening; it seems the moment that everybody has been waiting for has finally arrived. As the whispering increases, Sarah witnesses the arrival of a short, thin old man with thick, curly hair, delicately walking barefooted on the red carpet in the middle of the hall. He seems to be about five foot two or three inches tall and weighing 120 to 130 pounds. Wearing a long orange-colored robe that stretches all the way to his ankles, Baba seems to glide across the red carpet as the crowd cheers his arrival.

Sarah is also taken by Baba's appearance, but she is too curious about her surroundings. She wants to observe the crowd's reaction to Baba's presence. She notices a white middle-aged woman sitting next to her waving her arms in the air, like many other people in the hall, trying to push the air trapped in the hall towards her mouth as she breathes in heavily. Astonished by this act, Sarah asks the woman about her behavior. The woman, distracted by Sarah's untimely curiosity, warns her to stay quiet and instructs her to inhale Baba's energy. "Don't you see Baba oozing energy from his eyes? Try to fill your lungs with Baba's holy energy," the woman shouts. To better see Baba's face, Sarah attempts to stand, but a woman guard immediately orders her to sit.

Constantly turning his face toward the male and female visitors to the left and right of him, Sai Baba continues to walk along the red carpet, allowing the men and women to equally enjoy his presence. He does not say a word, gazing only upon his mesmerized audience, exchanging lingering glances with some. Some of those who are lucky enough to be in the front row closest to the red carpet hand Baba notes, saying things Sarah cannot hear from where she sits. Baba calmly accepts their notes, acknowledging their presence by moving his head toward them, staring into their eyes for a few fleeting moments.

Sarah now can easily hear her heart beating. As Sai Baba draws closer to where she is sitting, her heart begins to beat faster and faster. There are about 20 people separating Sarah from Baba; she wishes she were closer, so she could comfortably look into Baba's gentle eyes. All she wishes now is for Baba to bless her soul by looking into her eyes. It takes about ten minutes before the quiet old man walks, at last, to where Sarah is sitting. As Baba moves closer and closer, their eyes finally meet. With their eyes locked, it seems as if she cannot breathe. While she looks silently into the old man's dark, sunken eyes, Baba's sharp glance penetrates deep into her soul, filling her heart with happiness. Not wanting the moment to end, she continues staring at the old man's captivating eyes until Baba turns away. Cherishing those happy moments, Sarah closes her eyes, feeling energized.

A few minutes later, when she opens her eyes, Baba is gone and the guards begin ushering the audience toward the exit doors. As Sarah turns around, she sees the woman who was once sitting quietly behind her, holding her head in her hands, now shouting out of enthusiasm. "Did you see? Did you see?" she shouts out excitedly. "Today Baba looked at me and my life has changed, all my troubles are now behind me," she continues. "I made a wish that if Baba looked at me today, my life would turn around for good, and that's what happened. Did you see how Baba changed my destiny by the sacred energy of his glance?" she cries out in happiness. As Sarah quietly listens to the woman's exclamations, she reflects upon the seemingly limitless power of belief. Yet at the same time, she cannot help but hope that her visit will also change her life around for the better.

Sarah leaves the hall and walks along the pathways of the ashram. Now she can see the ashram in the daylight. Filled with tall trees and different vegetation, it is very green. She sits under the shade of a massive tree and contemplates her trip. The peaceful atmosphere of the ashram puts her in a sensitive mood; she whispers some verses from her favorite poet and thinks about her visit with Baba. She feels a bit disappointed about not noticing a significant change in her heart. It was all an observation to her, though a very interesting one. The new spiritual birth that she expected to happen did not occur. Is it too soon to see any changes, she wonders? Seeing others being so obviously moved by their visit makes her think that if something significant was going to happen, it would have happened by now.

The sun rises above the horizon, and the weather becomes more warm and humid. As she watches the passersby, she notices a lot of young people walking in groups. A little boy of about eight or nine years of age approaches her. He has his video camera in front of his face, filming. Sarah smiles; the boy, pretending to be a reporter, stands in front of her and in a mischievous tone asks: "Excuse me lady, can I ask your name? And what do you wish from Sai Baba?" Sarah laughs and answers: "Why don't you introduce yourself first?" To answer her, the boy moves the video camera aside, revealing his face. Sarah is shocked. The full smile that was covering her face a minute ago now freezes, and her tongue begins to stumble. The little boy has a very bizarre face. His bulging eyeballs look like they are coming out of their sockets, and his pupils are out of place and pointing in opposite directions. Instead of a nose, the boy has only two little holes above a tiny mouth, containing only one lip. It takes Sarah a few moments to take control of her emotions. The boy introduces himself as Pirouz and confides that he has come to be cured by Sai Baba. "My mom says that Baba will heal my face," the boy declares happily.

At lunchtime, Sarah walks toward the restaurant in the western wing of the ashram where many pilgrims meet one another. There, she sees the little boy again, this time accompanied by his mother. His mother, a very attractive young woman, introduces herself as Keshvar. As they get to know one another, Keshvar mentions she had a dream that someone cured her son. When she discussed her dream with her friends, they recommended that she take her son to Sai Baba's temple to seek a cure. Keshvar sounds very hopeful as she talks about taking her son to Baba. Sarah is amazed by the degree of confidence in the woman's voice. She speaks with such excitement that Sarah secretly wishes she could be present when the boy is cured. Yet, Sarah ponders, how can Sai Baba cure a face like that?

2

Miracle Child

If there is righteousness in the heart,
There will be beauty in the character.

If there is beauty in the character,
There will be harmony in the home.

When there is harmony in the home,
There will be order in the nation.

When there is order in the nation,
There will be peace in the world.

—Satya Sai Baba

The year 1926 was an auspicious one for the people of Puttaparthi, a village in the southern Indian province of Andhra Pradesh. It was in this year that, according to Hindu astrologers, a luminescent ball of light entered the side of Easwaramma, a pious village woman, and she was chosen by God to became the surrogate mother of a child who was to become the greatest living avatar of our age. Easwaramma and her husband, Pedda Venkappa Raju, lived a simple life and were known for their piety and respect for Hindu traditions and rites.

The village of Puttaparthi is nestled in a broad, deep valley with the Chitravati river running through it. This river empties into a tank (reservoir) that was built by an emperor centuries ago. A ring of majestic-looking pink-brown hills surrounds the valley. The village had once been the seat of a chieftain who had ruled over the surrounding area. The Raju family traced their family tree all the way back to that chieftain. Like their ancestors, they were respected by the villagers, and they continued to lead and guide their fellow villagers, particularly by teaching and training the youth. Pedda's father, Kondama Raju, was particularly known for his dedication to teaching and training the village youth.

Kondama was also greatly respected for his devotion to religious life and festivals. He was a great musician and actor, and participated in most of the religious festivals, dramas, and operas that were staged in Puttaparthi or nearby villages. He had a good voice and memorized most of the spiritual songs used during these festivals. The religious dramas were drawn from well-known spiritual epics such as the Ramayana, and they were the main source of entertainment for villages like Puttaparthi. To display his dedication to the Hindu gods, Kondama Raju dedicated a temple to the goddess Satyabhama, the consort of Lord Krishna. He gained the respect of his fellow villagers by this pious and generous act.

Easwaramma and her husband Pedda already had a son and two daughters, and they longed for another son. In Indian cultures, families strongly prefer sons, so if the next child were a son, that would have made them happy. All throughout her pregnancy, Easwaramma noticed that unusual things happened around their home. For example, the musical instruments that were left quietly leaning against the walls of her bedroom would suddenly, in the middle of the night, play without anybody touching them. She often pondered the meaning of these strange events. When she shared her observations with a Hindu priest known for his knowledge of the unseen, she was told that those events attested to the presence of a holy power in their house and the coming of an auspicious birth.

On November 23, 1926, as the sun showed its face from behind the pink-brown rocky hills of Puttaparthi and shone over the waters and sands of the Chitravati River, the sound of music filled the house of Easwaramma and her husband. Like at the birth of Buddha, during which elephants trumpeted in joy and peacocks danced, in the house of Easwaramma and Pedda, strange things happened: The twanging tambura and rhythmic meddela began playing by themselves, and with their sweet melody joyously heralded a special birth. The Lord, who was growing in the womb of Easwaramma, was about to make his earthly appearance.

The wait was finally over. As the night disappeared and day-light arrived, the child was born. Easwaramma's prayers had come true, and she had become the mother of a beautiful boy. The boy was named Satya-Narayana. *Satya* (or *Sathya*) in Sanskrit (the oldest known Indo-European language, spoken in ancient India) means "truth" or "reality," and *Narayana* is another name for Vishnu, the protective God of the Hindu trinity, to whom Easwaramma had prayed for a son. The three great Gods of Hinduism are Brahma, the creator; Vishnu, the protector; and Shiva (or Siva), the destroyer. It is a customary practice for Indians to name their children after the many gods whom they worship. According to Hindu astrologers, Satya's moment of birth coincided with a conjunction of supreme importance. According to Sai Baba's biographer Kasturi, a well-known Indian sage and yogi, Sri Aurobindo, had told of his vision of light crashing down from the stellar regions to the Earth in the region where the village of Puttaparthi was located.[3]

Another strange event during the birth of Satya-Narayana was the appearance of a cobra, the snake known as the lord of reptiles, in the child's bed. Women who attended his birth were surprised to witness an object moving under the child's bed-clothes. After removing the bedclothes, they found a coiled cobra lying next to the boy, without causing him any harm. The attendants interpreted the appearance of the cobra, a symbol of Lord Shiva, as a sign that the newborn was given multiple consecrations to the gods, especially to Shiva, and that the gods wanted to protect the infant from possible harm.

Cobras are not strangers to the people of Puttaparthi. In fact, the name *Puttaparthi* means "ant-hill place in which snakes live in the ant hills." According to an ancient legend, Puttaparthi once was a flourishing village with rich farmlands and healthy livestock, until a cobra was unwisely killed by local cowherds. Since then, the cobras cursed the region and its cowherds, causing the abundant farmlands to dry out and the cattle herds to diminish, and cobras became prolific. Today the region is known for having many cobras. Many snake shrines have been built to honor the Lord Shiva, and the region is also well known for its practitioners of sorcery and the black arts.

From birth, Satya was the talk of the village. Neighbors constantly admired him for his beauty, sweet smile, and good nature. He was unusually sincere, and compassionate toward all creatures, human or animal. His tender heart prevented him from eating meat. Unlike his young companions, who loved eating meat, he became a vegetarian at a very early age. He could not bear the suffering of animals. He avoided areas where animals were slaughtered or tortured. He did not even want to be in a kitchen in which meat was cooked and did not want to eat from the dishes that were used to serve meat. He avoided sports that involved animal cruelty, such as cock-fighting, bear-baiting, and bull-cart races.

Satya-Narayana often brought beggars and cripples home, and asked his mother or older sisters to feed them. This became a habit for him. One day his mother worried that they would not have enough food left for themselves, and warned Satya-Narayana that if she continued to give their food away, he would starve to death. The warning did not go well with Satya-Narayana, so he refused to eat and continued to offer his food to the needy in the village. Although his mother persuaded him to eat, the boy kept missing his meals. When his worried mother pleaded with him to eat, to his mother's surprise, he indicated that he had been fed by an old man with a certain name and

FOOD PRAYER
Selected from Sai Baba's Discourses

Three types of purities are said to be necessary with regard to food. These are 1. *Pathra Shuddhi* (purity of vessels): The vessels for cooking must be clean and pure. 2. *Paka Shuddhi* (purity of the process of cooking): The process of cooking should not bring impurities. The person who prepares the food and serves must not only be clean in dress, but also clean in habits, character, and conduct. He should not allow his mind to dwell on wicked or vicious ideas. 3. *Pachaka Shuddhi* (Purity of food materials): The provisions used for cooking [have] to be pure and of good quality. They should have been procured by fair means. The absence of any of the above three qualities makes the food impure. Impure food results in an impure mind. Hence it is necessary to purify the food before we eat.

Now it is not possible to ensure the purity of the cooking process, since we do not know what thoughts rage in the mind of the person who prepares the food. Similarly we cannot ensure cleanliness of the food ingredients, as we do not know whether the seller who had sold it to us acquired the food grains in a righteous way. Hence it is essential on our part to offer food to God in the form of a prayer, so that these three impurities do not afflict our mind. When we make the offering to God, all the three types of pollution are destroyed and the food is turned into *Prasad*, which will nourish us physically, mentally and spiritually.

characteristics, but neither his mother nor anyone else in the village knew a person with that name and characteristics. When his mother doubted his words, he put his hand, that he usually used for eating, in front of his mother's nose, and asked her to smell the balls of milk-rice that the old man had been feeding him. His mother could smell fresh milk-rice, and she believed the boy. She also could see that the boy did not display any sign of hunger, but continued his daily activities without any signs of weakness. She began to wonder if her son had mysterious contacts with unseen visitors from the world beyond her understanding.

Satya had a very close relationship with his paternal grand-father, Kondama Raju, a very spiritual man. He learned the ways of spirituality from him and acquired many of his grandfather's talents, such as singing, acting, and songwriting. By the time he reached his eighth birthday, he was writing songs for the village's spiritual plays. Like many children his age, Satya also attended the village school. Soon he began to outshine all his classmates with his ability to learn quickly. Because of his kind heart and entertaining nature, Satya made many friends. He showed up early for school and gathered his friends around him. He sang religious songs (*bhajans*), said prayers, and performed religious ceremonies, incorporating pictures of saints decorated with flowers.

Even children who were not interested in religious matters gathered around him because he could entertain them with his supernatural powers. One thing that made him very popular among his friends was Satya's ability to produce objects out of thin air. From an empty bag, he produced different kinds of fruits and flowers. He could even produce pencils and other school necessities for those who had lost theirs or who did not have resources to purchase any. His miraculous powers soon brought him popularity in the village of Puttaparthi and other nearby villages. People came from a distance to witness his miraculous power and see his magically created gifts. When his friends asked him about the source of his magical gifts, he mentioned a certain invisible "Grama Sakti," or powerful spirit-being, who obeyed his wishes and brought him what he desired.

Once in school, a teacher punished Satya unfairly by asking him to stand on a table for a long period of time. Satya used his supernatural powers to teach the teacher a lesson. After the class ended, the teacher wanted to get up from his chair to leave, but to his (and to witnessing students') amazement, he could not rise from his chair. It seemed that a massive force held him down. When he finally managed to stand up, the chair seemed to stick to him. As he helplessly struggled to remove himself from the chair, he thought about releasing Satya from his punishment. Immediately after he released Satya, he was able to free himself from the chair. This incident further spread Satya's reputation as a semidivine being.

For his high school education, Satya went to the town of Uravakonda, where his older brother was a teacher. His brother wanted him to finish high school and college and become a government officer. On the first day of school, Satya discovered that his reputation had reached the place long before he did. Everybody, teachers and students alike, was curious about his semidivine reputation and his magical powers. They knew him as a fine writer, good actor, dancer, and musician. He was known as a boy who was wiser than his teachers and who could peer into the past and see into the future. Others had also heard of his unique power of materializing objects out of nothing. He soon became the pet of the entire school, and the most popular student, whom everybody wanted to get closer to and know better. Different teachers looked for opportunities to have Satya in their classes. Because of his spiritual nature and his singing and acting abilities, he was assigned to lead the school prayer groups. Every morning, Satya, with his beautiful voice, inspired his fellow students, as well as his teachers, to achieve a good day of work.

Satya became the life and soul of the school. He was chosen by his drama teacher to be in charge of writing and producing a school play. Satya enthusiastically took over the task, and wrote a drama that became a great success. The play was called

Do Deeds Follow Words? and its theme was "hypocrisy." The hero of the play was a little boy who thoughtfully observed and pondered the behavior of people around him. Satya himself played the role of the boy.

The play opens with a seemingly respectable woman reading and explaining a selected number of verses from the *Bhagavata Purana* (an Indian legendary history) to a group of women who appear to be housewives. She emphasizes the importance of giving charity to truly needy people who have no other means of supporting themselves, not to healthy strong people who live idle lives and are not truly in need. Krishna, the boy, is sitting next to his mother and carefully listens to what his mother says to the women. As soon as the women disperse, a weak, blind beggar enters and seeks help, but is rebuked and turned away by his mother. Then a fat priest holding a polished copper vessel filled with grain in one hand and a richly ornamented musical instrument in the other hand enters the room. The mother cheerfully welcomes the man, and offers him rice and coins, then she falls on his feet and asks for forgiveness. When the man leaves, Krishna is perplexed by his mother's behavior and asks her why she did not act based on what she preached to the women arlier. His mother becomes irritated by the audacity of a boy who questions the ethics of adult behavior and says, "Can acts follow the words?" and drags the boy to his father's room.

The father, an accountant busy with his files, takes time to give Krishna a lecture about the value of education and hard work to overcome difficulties in the way of success in school. As he talks, a schoolboy pops in and asks for a rupee to pay his school fees in order to be allowed to show up for his classes and continue with his education. The father, unconcerned about the boy's education, tells him he has no money to help, and shows his empty handbag to prove the honesty of his statement. A few moments later, a group of well-dressed young accountants from the father's firm come in and request a contribution to put together a welcome dinner for an officer who would take charge of their office in a few days. Elated by the idea, the father pulls out a drawer in his desk, and gives the young men a large sum of money. He even offers to give a speech at the dinner to please the new officer. Appalled by this behavior, Krishna asks his father why he went against his own words and uttered a lie to the schoolboy. The father turns angry and says, "Should deeds follow words?" Then he shows his displeasure with the boy's questioning of his ethics by commanding him to go to school immediately.

The next scene takes place at the school. Krishna, together with other students, is listening to the teacher, who is worried about a visit by an inspector the next day. He instructs the students that if the inspector asks them how many lessons they have finished, they should say 32 instead of 23, which is the actual number of lessons they have finished. The teacher makes it clear that when the inspector comes, the class will go over lesson 33, one about King Harischandra, a righteous ruler who never uttered a lie. He goes over the lesson 33 repeatedly, making certain that the students can answer any possible questions asked by the inspector, and he threatens them with severe punishment if they show any indications that the lesson has already been reviewed in the class. When the class is dismissed, Krishna remains and asks the teacher a question, "Why do you not follow the advice you give? Why are you teaching us about the righteous king who never lied while you ask us to lie tomorrow?" Krishna receives from his teacher the same rebuff he received from his parents. Irritated by Krishna's questioning of his ethics, the teacher says, "Do you mean to say that the adviser should follow his advice?" "I am fed up with this hypocrisy, at home, at school, and everywhere," Krishna mutters.

The last scene in the play shows Krishna's home the next day. It is school time, but Krishna refuses to go. He displays his lack of interest in his education, and throws away his books, and states that school is a waste of precious time that could be used more efficiently. His distraught parents call for his teacher, and the teacher rushes in to convince the boy to go to school. When all of them, the teacher, the father, and the mother are present at one place, Krishna faces them and states, "If all that you instruct as mother, father, and teacher is only to be spoken and written, and if all that one learns is to be discarded when it comes to action, I do not understand why I should learn anything at all." This is the end of the play.

It is amazing that Satya was only 12 years old when he wrote and acted in this play. Satya wished that his play would help to open people's eyes to their shortcomings, so they might learn to speak the truth in such a way that their deeds would follow their words.

3

Challenges
of Childhood

Truth is the mother
Wisdom is the father
Right conduct is the brother
Compassion is the friend
Peace is the spouse
Forgiveness is the son
These six alone are the real relations for every one.

—Satya Sai Baba

atya's reputation as a boy with supernatural powers grew. He gave new life to village religious rites and spiritual plays by his talented acting, singing, and dancing. Because of his small physique and his acting versatility, especially his ability to change the tone of his voice, he could play both male and female roles. It was not unusual for Satya to play both genders, since in rural India girls usually did not take part in religious plays, and boys did most of the acting. As a versatile actor, Satya often assumed more than one role in the same play. Because of his unique talents, charismatic personality, and spiritual character, Satya could credibly perform gods in legends. Gods and demons were the main characters of Indian village religious plays and operas, and religious legends were the main themes. One night when he was playing the role the man-lion avatar Narasimha Deva, he acted as if he was truly the lion-god. He leaped like a lion, and transformed his face into such ferocity, rage, and benediction that the audience was gravely frightened. According to witnesses, that night Narasimha Deva manifested himself through the boy and took over Satya's body. It required the strength of several strong men to hold and calm the boy, as he had the strength of ten men, according to the claims of observers. Eventually, the boy was pacified when some in the audience conducted a traditional act of worship that was usually given to the lion-god Narasimha Deva.[4]

It soon became obvious that something was different about Satya. There were many signs that indicated the boy had connections with supernatural beings. He won the respect of people in surrounding villages for his knowledge of the unseen and for his use of knowledge for good causes. Once a man who had lost his horse, one he used for pulling his cart, came to Satya to ask him to locate his horse. He was desperate because he had looked everywhere and had not found the animal. Satya kindly directed the man to a certain area near the town. The man followed Satya's direction, and to his pleasure and amazement found his horse calmly grazing. The man was so pleased by Satya's help that he and his friends often offered Satya a ride to or from school. They sincerely believed that the boy's presence would bring them grace and good fortune.

At the age of 13, Satya's life was completely changed by an incident that shocked the entire town of Uravakonda. On March 8, 1940, around 7:00 P.M., while Satya was walking barefoot on the hillsides of Uravakonda, his friend heard him scream violently. When friends reached him, they found him leaping up and down grasping one of his right foot's toes and screaming. The first thing that came to mind was that he had been stung by one of the black scorpions that were known to live in the area. His friends looked for the scorpion or a serpent but could not find any in the dusk. They became very worried about Satya's health because according to local superstitious belief, no one could survive the bite of a scorpion or a snake in Uravakonda. The word *Uravakonda,* in fact, means "serpent hill" (*urava* or *uraga* mean "serpent," and *konda* means "hill"). The town Uravakonda derives its name from the hill that dominates the area. A huge boulder, about 100 feet high, crowns the hill and gives it the shape of a many-hooded serpent that has raised its head, ready to strike with poisonous fangs.

Although there was no sign of a scorpion sting or snakebite, Satya's condition worsened. He fell unconscious, and his body became stiff, as if he were lifeless. His friends became worried about him; they did know what caused his condition. Some thought that a demonic spirit known as Muthyalamma, who supposedly lived in the cave of Uravakinda, had taken possession of Satya's body, so they went into the cave and offered sacrifices to the demon spirit by laying before it flowers, coconuts, and burning incense.

When Satya's brother Seshama heard the news, he brought with him a doctor who gave Satya an injection and some medicine. After a few days, Satya began to regain consciousness, but he was now a different person. His parents, traveling from Puttaparthi, soon joined him. They were shocked to see the changes in Satya; they hardly recognized him. He did not eat, nor did he answer those who spoke to him. He was silent most of the time but occasionally burst into song and recited poetry. Often his body became stiff, and he looked as if his spirit had left his body. When he was conscious, his moods changed intermittently from laughter to weeping. Sometimes he recited long religious verses and passages in Sanskrit, far beyond what he had learned through his education and training. Words of wisdom poured from his mouth and astonished those around him. He talked about pilgrimage places he had never visited. He spoke philosophical thought as if he had studied philosophy for decades.

Satya's behavior became more and more mysterious. Though he seemed to be unconscious, he was well aware of events surrounding him. One day he asked his parents to go to the next house and bring to him a scholar who was there and was misinterpreting the Sanskrit books of epics. The scholar did not believe that the boy possessed insight into the unseen and refused to come.

Finally, when Satya's parents acted desperate and begged him to please indulge the sick child by a short visit, he agreed. When the scholar arrived, he and Satya engaged in a serious discourse about the correct usage and interpretation of the text. The scholar was overwhelmed by Satya's depth of knowledge about the religious text and by his supernatural powers; he fell at Satya's feet and apologized for not coming sooner, humiliated by the omniscient boy.

Although more doctors were consulted, Satya's condition did not improve. The symptoms of laughter and weeping, eloquence and silence remained the same. People suggested different causes, and cures, for the boy's afflictions, but what many agreed upon was the idea that a demon spirit possessed the boy. The solution was deemed to lie in the hands of an exorcist, whom Satya's brother brought to the house. When he saw the exorcist, Satya faced him and commanded, "Come on! You have been worshipping me every day, and now that you have come here, your only business is to worship me and clear out." After he heard the boy, the exorcist left in a hurry and forgot to collect his fee. He advised the brother to treat the boy respectfully because of his divine connections.

Satya's condition still did not improve, and his parents took him back to Puttaparthi and watched his behavior closely. His statements amazed them. For example, he would say to his sisters, "Here, wave the sacred lamp, the gods are passing across the sky." He noticed that his parents worried about his health, and he told them, "Why do you worry like this? There will be no doctor there when you go, and even if one is there, he cannot cure me."[5] His parents still thought that their son's illness was the result of someone's black magic, and that the boy's body had been possessed by demon spirits, and they finally decided to take him to an exorcist in the nearby village of Brahmanapalli, near Kadiri, who was known for the torturous treatment of his patients.

This exorcist was a man of gigantic stature, with blood-red eyes and untamed behavior. According to those who knew the man, he was a "powerful practitioner before whom no evil spirit dared wag its poisonous tail." They believed that he would cure Satya and soon send him back to school. First, the sorcerer performed a rite in which a chicken and a lamb were sacrificed, and he made Satya sit in the center of a circle of their blood while he chanted strange incantations. His exorcism soon became a contest of willpower between himself and the indifferent Satya, who laughed at his repeated failures. Unsuccessful, he experimented with desperate and dangerous techniques that more resembled medieval torture than a healing ritual. He shaved Satya's head, and used a sharp object to score several crosses on his scalp from the top of his head to his forehead. The cuts were so deep that the blood flowed. Then he poured lime juice, garlic and other acidic fruits on his bleeding scalp. He wanted to make the body of his patient suffer so brutally that the excess pain would draw out the occupying demon, but his attempts were to no avail. Satya patiently sat through the torture without flinching or showing any signs of pain.

Furious with the boy's lack of response, the exorcist tried other methods from his repertory of torture. Every morning for several days he poured 108 pots of cold water on Satya's wounded scalp. Since this still did not produce the desired result, he used other tortures, such as beating the boy in his joints with a heavy stick in order to chase the demon out of him. As his options ran out, the exorcist decided to use his strongest weapon, one he was certain even the toughest of spirits could not withstand. He experimented with a "Kalikam," a mixture of acidic liquids, collyrium (eye salve), and the most fiery abracadabras (incantations) from his repertoire of torment. He applied the mixture to Satya's eyes in the hope this would produce the desired results.[6]

Satya's parents and older sister watched all these torturous practices. The parents were horrified by this experimentation. The mixture caused Satya's face and head to swell beyond recognition. His eyes shrunk to thin tear-exuding slits, and his body shook under the impact of pain. His parents and sister witnessed the amount of pain their beloved Satya endured and wept in anguish and tried to console him whenever the exorcist was not paying attention to him. Satya made signs that he wanted his parents and sister to remain quiet. He gestured that they should leave the room and he would join them later. After he made an excuse to the exorcist, Satya left the room and told his parents how to make a remedy for the swelling. This was secretly prepared by his parents and applied to Satya's eyes. His eyes, which had been reduced to two narrow slits, widened again, and the swelling gradually subsided. When the exorcist learned that Satya's parents had interfered, he was enraged. He claimed that he was within an inch of victory and that they had ruined his results. They paid him his fees and gave him gifts, and told him they would return the boy for further torment after they had built up his stamina. They sneaked the boy away from the exorcist and his torture chamber, and took him back to Puttaparthi.

When he was back in Puttaparthi, Satya's bizarre behavior remained the same. His moods continued to fluctuate. Sometimes he seemed to have the strength of ten men, and sometimes he was as weak and fragile as a lotus stalk. He continued reciting poetry and praising the Lord. He spoke of the evils of hypocrisy and revealed the inner secrets of adults around him. His parents tried other doctors, but their efforts were in vain. It had been a while since Satya had left his high school in Uravakonda, but it

WHO IS THE REAL GURU?
Selected from Sai Baba's Discourses

The true meaning of *Guru* is "one who dispels darkness of ignorance." *Gu* means "darkness of ignorance" and *Ru* means "one who removes." Another meaning for *Guru* is "one who reveals the *Guri* (target) to the disciple." He does this by removing the darkness of ignorance. *Guri* here refers to the *Atmic* principle present in every human being. The real Guru who can reveal the *Atmic* principle is a *Jnaanamurthy* (embodiment of wisdom); He is the very embodiment of Divine principles; and He is one who takes upon Himself a form to teach the same to the disciple; he is God Himself.

Another meaning of the word *guru* is "one who is beyond attributes and forms." *Gu* stands for *Gunaatheetha*—one who transcends the three *Gunas* (*Satva, Rajas* and *Thamas*); *Ru* stands for *Rupavarjitha*—one who is formless. The One who is beyond all attributes and forms is none other than the Supreme Self (the *Brahman*) who is resident within each of us. Only God can be regarded as One who is beyond attributes and forms.

Guru is Brahma, who is the Creator of the universe. Guru is Vishnu who is all-pervasive and is also the Doer in the universe. Guru is *Maheshvara* who commands and ordains everything in the universe in the right manner. Guru is not one who merely teaches. A real Guru is Omnipotent, Omniscient, and Omnipresent, He is God Himself.

There is only one Guru, that is God and there is no other Guru. We have to recognize Him as our only preceptor. He is the preceptor of preceptors. Realizing that God dwells within us, we must treat God as the universal Guru and the preceptor for mankind and contemplate on Him.

Let us purify our hearts to let the Divine dwell in it. Let us install God in our hearts. The vibrations that emanate from the heart will elevate us and confer Divine Wisdom on us.

Source: *http://www.eaisai.com/baba/*.

did not seem that any change was forthcoming. Satya's family watched him go through his bizarre metamorphosis with anguish and wonderment, until an event happened on May 23, 1940, that ended his period of aberrant behavior.

On May 23, more than two months after he first fell unconscious, Satya called the members of his household to gather around him. His parents shared the house with his siblings, so there were always many children around his age present. Out of thin air, Satya, with wave of his hand, produced sugar candy and flowers for his family members. Soon the neighbors heard that Satya had materialized objects and rushed in. A crowd gathered around him like they did before his crisis, and Satya seemed to be in a joyful mood, similar to the demeanor he exhibited before his sickness. He distributed more sugar candy and flowers, and later out of love and appreciation for the crowd provided each person with a ball of rice-milk (rice cooked in milk).

The news reached Satya's father, Pedda. He arrived, and squeezed his way through the crowd around him. The crowd asked him to wash his feet, hands, and face before approaching the divine Giver of Boons. This angered him, and he thought of finding a way to put an end to the boy's antics. According to Satya's biographer, N. Kasturi, the father did not seem impressed by how his child materialized objects, and at the time he thought that Satya tricked everybody by hiding things and pretending to produce them, by sleight of hand. All he wanted was a normal child, like every other child. He stood before his 13-year-old son and shouted, "This is too much, it must stop." He waved a stick in his hand and threatened to beat the bizarre behavior out of his son. Again he shouted, "Are you a God, or a ghost, or a mad-cap? Tell me!" Satya responded to his father's wrath by calmly responding, "I am Sai Baba."[7]

The Road to Godhood

Love in thought is truth.
Love in action is right conduct.
Love in understanding is peace.
Love in feeling is non-violence.

—Satya Sai Baba

No one in the crowd had heard of anyone named "Sai Baba." Like the crowd, Satya's father was stunned into silence after he heard the boy's claim of a new identity. "Who was Sai Baba?" he thought to himself. Sai Baba said, "I belong to Apastamba Sutra, the school of Sage Apastamba, and I am of the spiritual Lineage of Bharadwaja. I am Sai Baba. I have come to ward off all your troubles, and to keep your houses clean and pure," the boy continued. At this point, his brother Seshama approached him and asked, "What do you mean by claiming to be Sai Baba?" Satya did not answer this question, but stated "Your Venkavadhootha prayed that I would be born in your family, so I came." The crowd asked Seshama about Venkavadhootha. He described Venkavadhootha as one of their forefathers who had been a pious sage and who had been looked upon as a guru by hundreds of villagers in the area.[8]

Out of curiosity about Satya's new identity, his family inquired around nearby villages, and someone suggested that a certain pious government officer, who lived in the nearby village of Penukonda, was an ardent devotee and follower of a hermit Muslim sage known as Sai Baba of Shirdi. Satya's parents thought this man would be able to help them understand their son's new identity and possibly shed some light on the boy's strange behavior. After some reluctance, the man agreed to see Satya. When he saw Satya, the man suggested that Satya's case was a clear case of mental derangement, and that he needed to be taken to a mental institution for treatment. When he heard the man's words, Satya said, "Yes, it is mental derangement, but whose? You are but a blind servant. You cannot recognize the very Sai whom you have been worshipping!"[9] Then Satya waved his hand, and out of nothing he produced a handful of ash-like powder (*vibhuti*) and scattered it in all directions.

Although reincarnation is a basic component of Hindu belief, Satya's parents could not easily accept that their son was a reincarnation of Sai Baba of Shirdi, who had died in 1918. They required better proof of such a reincarnation. The old government officer, who was a dedicated devotee of Sai Baba of Shirdi, also could not easily accept that this boy with his wild behavior was his spiritual master's actual reincarnation. Satya's father, who felt he did not get enough help from the old man, assumed that Sai Baba of Shirdi might speak through the boy, so he asked Satya, "What are we to do with you?" Satya swiftly answered, "Worship Me every Thursday! Keep your minds and houses pure."[10] The visit did not clarify Satya's claim and mental status.

Satya's parents soon learned more about the life and deeds of Sai Baba of Shirdi, whom their son claimed to be. They knew that he was a pious man who had lived about 60 years earlier in the village of Shirdi, in northern India, until his death in 1918. According to his followers, Sai Baba of Shirdi was endowed with unprecedented powers, which he used to heal the sick, protect the vulnerable, avert lethal accidents by his timely intervention, and help spiritual seekers with their spiritual growth and evolution. Although during his life Sai Baba of Shirdi repeatedly made it clear that he was only a simple man, many of his devotees nevertheless regarded him as an avatar, and some even worshiped him. Being an ardent devotee, the old Indian officer also considered Sai Baba of Shirdi his God-incarnated guru. According to many accounts of his life, Sai Baba of Shirdi was a Muslim, but he emphasized that his teachings and blessings were for all, regardless of their religious affiliation, caste, or creed.

Thursdays in Hindu India are traditionally reserved for the veneration of gurus. On a Thursday following Satya's visit to Penukonda, as the crowd gathered around Satya, someone in the audience challenged him to show some new proof that he was truly Sai Baba, as he claimed to be. Satya agreed to do so. The crowd awaited another miracle and gathered closer to witness Satya's new display of supernatural power. Satya said, "Place in my hands those jasmine flowers," When they did so, he threw the flowers on the floor, and to the audience's surprise and astonishment, the flowers fell harmoniously, spelling the name *SAI BABA* in Telugu script, the local language of the area. To those who could read, there was no doubt about the clarity and accuracy of the words' arrangement.[11]

As time passed, people began to question Satya's condition of "mental derangement," as proclaimed by the old government officer of Penukonda, and they started to accept him more and more as the god-man he claimed to be. The significant events of his life, such as materializing objects out of thin air and the embodiment of gods (as happened during the spiritual plays), his ability to journey out of his body during pain and suffering (as happened in the hands of the cruel exorcist), and his production of the sacred ash known as *vibhuti*, as well as other miracles here and there, began to make more sense for his observers as acts of a divine being.

SAI BABA OF SHIRDI

Sai Baba of Shirdi was known for his simple spiritual philosophy and tolerance of different religious traditions. His mission was to restore belief in God among his followers and to instill in them love and righteousness. Both Hindus and Muslims today claim him as one of their own saints. He did much in his life to bring the two religious groups together to form a single spiritual human community. Though he never called himself a guru, today he has millions of devotees who consider him to be their guru and who believe that he will always appear as their savior in moments of crisis.

The accounts of his early life are still a mystery, but it is believed that he was born in 1835 in Pathri, in Marathwada, in central India. He later moved to Shirdi in Maharashtra in Northern India. After years of wandering in forests, he found a permanent refuge in a dilapidated mosque that he referred to it as "Dwarkamai" (named after the abode of Krishna, Dwarka). His mosque, although an Islamic building, was open to all regardless of religion, caste or creed.

He was a very compassionate man, and whatever he earned he shared with the poor or sick and others in need. His spiritual powers, compassion, simplicity, and lack of interest in material gain created an aura of reverence among the spiritual seekers. Although he dissuaded people from worshiping him, his divine energy nevertheless touched the hearts of many who came to accept him as a true avatar and embodiment of God, and as their spiritual master and savior. According to some of his devotees, before his death on October 15, 1918, he foretold that he would be reborn eight years later.

At his parents' request and persistence, Satya agreed to go back to Uravakonda to live with his older brother Seshama and to continue his high school education. The incidents of his transition, and the emergence of his new personality, made Satya even more an object of curiosity and puzzlement for his classmates and teachers at Uravakonda. He was considered by some to be a child prophet and by others to be a mysterious prodigy. His teachers and fellow students often tested his intellectual and spiritual acuity. To their admiration, there was no question from his teachers that he could not answer properly. His intellectual talents matched his spiritual capacity. Many, including the headmaster of the school, became reverent and ardent believers in him.

Thursdays became a major event in the town of Uravakonda. In his brother's house, Satya received many visitors from Uravakonda and neighboring villages who brought him flowers, fruits, and sweets, and listened to his inspiring words of wisdom. He materialized items that linked him to his former incarnation as Sai Baba of Shirdi. To his followers' bewilderment, he materialized photographs, drawings, and paintings of Sai Baba of Shirdi, pieces of the clothing that Sai Baba of Shirdi wore, dates and fruits offered by his followers at the Shirdi shrine, and vibhuti or sacred ash powder, which gradually became his signature mark.

Sometime in October of 1940, in response to an invitation by some city servants, Seshama took his brother Satya to visit Hospet. Hospet was a town known for containing the ruins of Hampi, the capital of ancient Vijayanagara, a famous Indian empire, within its vicinity. Seshama hoped that a change of atmosphere might help Satya to regain his mental stability. While they visited the ruins of Hampi, the group approached the temple dedicated to Virupaksha, the patron deity of the empire. Although everyone else entered the temple, Satya sat outside and admired the architecture. As the others entered the temple, the priest who guided the group asked the visitors to look for the statue of a well-known deity inside the shrine. Inside the shrine they saw, to their astonishment, not a statue of a deity, but an image of Satya, who stood tall and smiling. Some in the group thought that Satya had gotten inside before them to trick them, and they rushed outside to look for him. There they found Satya in solitude, leaning against the wall and contemplating the distant horizon. "How can he be in two places simultaneously?" they wondered. At this, many in the group acknowledged Satya's divine status and claims, and some worshipped him in a way reserved only for gods. The next day, he puzzled the group further when he cured a patient suffering from chronic tuberculosis by his touch. The patient stood up and walked like a healthy person. The news of the trip soon spread, and Satya attracted more devotees.

As Satya became more popular and gathered more followers, he felt it was necessary to leave school, which he thought did not further his educational growth, in order to reach out instead to those who needed his help and wisdom. On October 20, 1940, Satya returned home from school, threw away his books, and proclaimed, "I am no longer your Satya. I am Sai." According to a later interview with his sister-in-law, who was present on that day, a bright halo surrounded Satya's head and almost blinded her with its splendor. Satya addressed her, "I am going, I don't belong to you, maya (illusion) has gone, My devotees are call-ing Me, I have My work, I cannot stay any longer." His brother Seshama, who still had not accepted Satya's new identity, pleaded with him to stop his madness, but Satya responded, "Give up all your efforts to cure Me. I am Sai. I do not consider Myself related to you."[12] A neighbor who had witnessed the conversation later claimed that he too saw the halo around Sai's head; he then fell at Sai's feet and accepted his divine nature. Later on, some other followers saw the same halo, and it became another source of enchantment among his devotees.

In spite of Seshama's pleas to stay, Sai left the house to pursue his divine work of answering his devotees' calls. October 20, 1940, became known as the day that Sai officially renounced his family name and declared himself to be Sai Baba. He moved into an ardent devotee's house, which was a spacious bungalow, and received his visitors in a beautiful garden amidst colorful flowers and trees. Unlike his brother's house, this large house was a suitable place for holding his routine gatherings and for the performance of rituals of worship that included singing in chorus the prayers that he had taught his followers. The news of Sai's departure from school left many of his classmates in tears, because they knew that he would now be far beyond their reach. In order to see him they must now wait among the long lines of devotees who wish to view the God-incarnate Sai.[13]

The devotional songs and hymns (*bhajans*) that Sai taught to his devotees became popular and were used during the prayer sessions. In his first bhajan, he invited the spiritual seekers to worship God, who has chosen him as his Earthly embodiment: "Oh, ye seekers! Worship the Feet of the Guru, with all your mind; you can thus cross the ocean of grief and joy, and birth and death."[14]

He invited his devotees to accept him as their God in their hearts and minds rather than in their words. He also made connections between his divine mission and major Indian gods such as the Lord Shiva:

> O Mind, without worshiping the Lotus Feet of Guru Sai Natha it is not possible to cross the ocean of life and death. Victory to the Noble Teacher, Lord Sai Natha. Chant "Om Namah Shivaya." Chant the name of Lord Shiva, Who resides in Arunachala (a sacred mountain in Southern India associated with Lord Shiva). Chant the name of Lord Baba, Whose form is Om.[15]

According to his devotees, an incident that happened during one of these gatherings in the garden confirmed Satya's new identity and convinced many more people to believe in his divine connections. A photographer who wanted to get a clear picture of Satya asked him to change position, as he was standing in front of a rock, which would have spoiled the picture. Satya did not pay attention, so the photographer took the picture anyway, hoping for the best. Later on, as he developed the film, he noticed that instead of the obstructing rock there was an image of Sai Baba of Shirdi. To his amazement, and to those who were present at the gathering and later saw the picture, the rock was nothing but Sai Baba of Shirdi participating in the gathering.

One evening after he had renounced his family and announced the beginning of his divine mission, Satya suddenly noticed his mother Easwaramma in the crowd that had gathered in the garden. Pointing to his mother, he stated, "Oh, maya has come!" ("The illusion is presenting itself.") By this, he referred to his past as Satya as part of illusion and his present as Sai Baba as reality. A few days later, his parents encouraged him to go back to Puttaparthi. They promised that they would not interfere with his mission and that they would respect his new identity. After a few days of staying with his parents and uncle, Satya moved to the house of the village accountant, Karnum, whose wife, Subbamma, was his ardent devotee. The Karnum family was also of the Brahman caste and known for their good deeds. They often fed Satya vegetable meals when he declined the meat meals in his parents' house. The house of the Brahman family was much more spacious and comfortable than his parents' cottage for receiving his daily visitors.

5

Establishment of Divinity

My work is ceaseless and so your work too is without end.
Know that I am within you and without you.
There is no difference. Rid yourselves of petty matters.
You are now ME and I am now THEE. There is no difference.
My Darshan will pour forth from ME to and through you.
You may be unaware of this constant action.
Be ever pure in heart and soul, and mankind in your
lifetime will benefit from your unique qualities.

—Satya Sai Baba

The road to godhood had become much smoother for Satya. Since he assumed the name Sai Baba, his devotees stopped calling him by his given name, Satya-Narayana, and started addressing him as Sai Baba. His new name derived from his former incarnation, Sai Baba of Shirdi, and attested to his God-incarnate quality (hence he will be referred to as Sai Baba for the remainder of this book). Some also called him Bala Sai (meaning Boy Sai). Soon, his reputation as God-incarnate reached to faraway villages. People rushed from all over to see the holy boy of Puttaparthi.

Visitors could no longer wait for Thursdays, the traditional day in India for honoring gurus, so they came as they pleased, and Sai Baba received them daily on an informal basis, sometimes twice a day. The house of the village accountant, where Sai Baba was staying, contained a relatively large prayer hall, which was the major feature of the building, and it was used for communal chanting. Since Sai Baba insisted on feeding his visitors, they had to build a dining hall as well. His followers began to attribute some Solomon-like qualities to Sai Baba. According to some women who served at the dining hall, whenever the food was not sufficient enough to feed all the visitors, Sai Baba used his divine power to increase the quantity of food. He would strike two coconuts (which are a fixed feature of Hindu celebrations and rituals) against each other to break them in half, and then he would sprinkle the juice in the food vessels. His holy intervention increased the quantity of the food, so everybody present could have enough to eat.

As the number of daily visitors increased, there was need for more space and accommodations, so sheds and tents were put up around his residence. Visitors who knew about the space limitations brought their own tents and lodging equipment. One way to overcome the limited space was to take the devotees to the open sands of the Chitravati River, where they said prayers and performed spiritual rituals under the blue sky. Sai Baba and his followers often gathered together in the evenings and chanted spiritual songs until the dark hours of the night. Sai Baba also advised his followers about their personal problems and helped them with their spiritual growth and to live a righteous life.

Based on his devotees' requests, Sai Baba often showed them a vision of his former life as Sai Baba of Shirdi. He would hold out his open palms and display shining images of himself on one palm and Shirdi's on the other. His devotees could even sometimes, upon request, view the glowing three-dimensional figure of Sai Baba of Shirdi in the corner of their rooms. One of Sai Baba's female devotees described her vision with the following words: ". . . there sat Shirdi Sai Baba on the floor in his characteristic pose, but with his eyes closed and ash marks on his forehead and arms. The incense sticks before him were burning, and the smoke was rising straight into the air. His body was glowing with strange effulgence, and there was a beautiful fragrance around him."[16]

Satya Sai Baba referred to Sai Baba of Shirdi as "My previous body." While explaining his divine mission for humanity, he compared himself to Lords Rama and Krishna, who had come to restore divine Truth, Morality, Peace, and Love, and to instill faith in God among those who denied him because of pride and ignorance, as well as to save the good from the claws of the bad. When questioned about his appearance in the form of Satya Sai Baba, he said "If I had come amongst you as Narayana with four arms holding the conch, the wheel, the mace and the lotus [emblems of divine powers], you would have kept Me in a museum and charged a fee for those who seek darshan [seeing and experiencing a saint for blessing]; if I had come as a mere man, you would not have respected My teaching and followed it for your own good. So, I have to be in this human form with supra-human wisdom and powers."[17]

While he lived in Subbamma's house, Sai Baba would frequently disappear into the hills that surrounded the village. He was often found sitting on a rock overlooking the village in a state of contemplation, or he was found in a cave, or sitting on the sands of the Chitravathi River.

Sai Baba was known for his playful nature. As his age naturally required, he loved to play outside with his friends and occasionally played jokes and tricks on them. Sai Baba later explained the first 16 years of his life as characterized mainly by *lila* (or *leela*), meaning "sport" and "play." His friends often followed him to the crest of a rocky hill at the bank of the river, where a lone tamarind tree stood. The tree was known as the "wish-fulfilling tree" because of its divine attributes. Sai Baba and his friends climbed the tree, and when they were playing in the midst of leaves and branches, Sai Baba often asked them to name their favorite fruits. To their astonishment, Sai Baba picked their desired fruits from the branches of the tamarind tree and handed them to them. His friends witnessed Sai Baba conjuring a variety of fruits, including apples, pears, mangoes, grapes, bananas, oranges, figs, and even fruits that were out of season or did not grow in the area. Sai Baba's power, according to his devotees, made the solitary tamarind tree a true "wish-fulfilling tree."

Other strange events happened around the tree on the rocky hill. Sai Baba often challenged his friends to race him to the top of the hill. His friends, before being able to take a few steps, found Sai Baba at the top of the hill standing next to the tree and calling to them in a playful voice. They could not believe that a person with earthly physical power could climb a steep, sometimes near vertical, hill that quickly. One of his friends, who at the time was a college student, later told Howard Murphet, the author of *Sai Baba: Man of Miracles*, what he saw as he was competing against Sai Baba to reach the top of the hill. He said, "With evening closing in, suddenly a great ball of fire like a sun pierced the dusk around the youth on the crest. The light was so bright it was impossible to keep your eyes open and watch it. About three or four of the devotees fainted and fell."[18] Other Sai Baba devotees who were interviewed by Howard Murphet reported more miracles involving lights on the rocky hill. Murphet wrote, "Different visions are said to have been seen on different occasions. Sometimes it was a great fiery wheel or a full moon with Baba's head in the center, sometimes a pillar of fire."

Sai Baba's devotees who spent time with him during his youth often talk about his playful nature. Murphet has interviewed a devotee of Sai Baba who was a successful businessman in Madras at the time of the interview. The devotee spent a whole month with Sai Baba in the early 1940s and witnessed Sai Baba's playful nature and his miracles. He told Murphet, "All the time in those days Baba was full of laughter and fun. He would sing songs, and many times a day he would perform some miracle, often as a prank, such as making a clock run backwards, or holding people to their seats by some invisible force. At picnics he would tap empty dishes, and when the lids were removed, the dishes would be full of food, sometimes hot as if straight from the kitchen. I have also seen him multiply small amounts of food to feed big crowds." [19]

The news of these and other miracles concerning Sai Baba traveled to Madras and other faraway places, and people came to see the miracle boy. Some of the devotees of the deceased Sai Baba of Shirdi heard of his reincarnation in Puttapathi, so they rushed to see him in his new residence. Others came as curious individuals to find out about this miracle boy about whom everybody talked. It was not an easy journey to Puttaparthi. The visitors had to travel for hours along an arduous road by bullcart or on foot. They all came from different walks of life. Among them were educators, clerks, merchants, doctors, and lawyers. These all thronged to Subbamma's house, where Sai Baba met his visitors.

As Sai Baba's devotees multiplied, Subbamma' house and new additions became too small to accommodate the needs of visitors. In 1944, a temple was built at the edge of the village. The new building was primarily a prayer temple. It was a simple building with a galvanized iron roof and was large enough to provide space for visitors. Rooms toward the back of the building were used as lodging spaces for devotees who had come from faraway places. Older devotees today speak of the old temple, which is known as the "Old Mandir," in a nostalgic tone. It holds historical value for those who visit Sai Baba in his new temple. Today, the walls of the old temple are covered by unique old photographs that show young Sai Baba and his early devotees. During those years when Sai Baba was not as popular as he is today, it was easier for devotees to spend high-quality time with him. He composed many songs and hymns about the love of God, a topic about which he affectionately taught his devotees,

WHAT IS AN ASHRAM?

An ashram is the residence of a spiritual master (*guru*) who meets and teaches spiritual seekers. This tradition has existed in India for centuries. The dwelling-place itself may be a cave, an open pavilion with a roof, a tiny one-person hut, or an enormous complex of buildings. Some ashrams accommodate visitors, and others accommodate only the master or guru. Some ashrams are open to all, and some are open only to the devotees, followers, and supporters of a particular spiritual guide.

An ashram is traditionally a place for retreat. People usually do not live in an ashram while they conduct their daily business and earn a livelihood and raise a family. There are exceptions, of course, but most ashrams are places of intense study, practice, and devotion. Ashrams are meant to serve as places of tranquil retreat from the demands of the world; they are usually established in quiet, rural areas where the residents' tranquility and meditations will not be severely disturbed. Like monasteries, many ashrams function as schools by offering education to children and also as relief centers by serving as points for the collection, preparation, and distribution of food to the local poor. Some visitors may stay in an ashram for a few days, and others may stay for their entire lives.

Some of the most famous ashrams in India are the Sabarmati Ashram in Ahmedabad, which was the headquarters for Mahatma Gandhi, and the Aurobindo Ashram in Pondicherry, which was the center for the work of the Bengali sage Sri Aurobindo Ghosh. Given the affluence of some of their Western visitors, some modern ashrams in India, like Prasanthi Nilayam (Sai Baba's ashram), now resemble vacation resorts more than the traditional ashrams of India.

and trained them to direct their spiritual devotion to helping people in need. The temple was the scene of countless transformations of character, revolutions in belief, confirmations of faith, curing of disease, calming of temper, discarding of hatred, salvaging of souls and reunions of hearts.

By the late 1940s, even the old temple seemed inadequate to meet the needs of the rapidly increasing number of visitors. Sai Baba's influential devotees included government officials and people of financial means, and they built an ashram for Sai Baba. They incorporated the ashram as a separate township in itself, so Sai Baba would be free from the petty antagonisms of minor village officials. Sai Baba called the new building complex *Prasanthi Nilayam*, which means "Abode of Peace."

During the construction of Prasanthi Nilayam, Subbamma, Sai Baba's old faithful devotee, fell ill. She was taken to Bukkapatnam, where a relative took care of her. Despite her illness, one day she still managed to come back to Puttaparthi by bullcart to see the progress in the building of the temple. In Puttaparthi, she was saddened to hear that Sai Baba was in Bangalore. A relative advised her that she should forget about Sai Baba, who was miles away at the time, and concentrate on her immediate family, who were around her. Still, she was certain that Sai Baba would come to see her before she left this earthly domain. She was resting in her deathbed at Bukkapatnam while Sai Baba was away on a mission. After a long struggle, she seemed to have had her last breath, but a peculiar glow on her face stopped the relatives from removing her body for a traditional Hindu cremation. Some wise people around her advised the others that they should respect the old woman's wish to see her guru, Sai Baba, before they pronounced her dead. After the announcement of Subbamma's death, her body was placed on the floor because of the belief that no Hindu should die upon a bed. Some relatives began to reveal their impatience and displeasure with the decision to wait for Sai Baba. After three days, Sai Baba finally returned. He sat by her, and gently called her twice, "Subbamma, Subbamma." To the crowd's astonishment,

Subbamma, whom everybody assumed was dead, suddenly opened her eyes and extended her hand toward Sai Baba. She firmly grasped Sai Baba's hand and began to stroke it affectionately. Sai Baba gently put his fingers to her lips. Her mouth opened a little, and the crowd felt that Sai Baba was giving her something to satisfy her soul's thirst. According to N. Kasturi, who narrated the story, "From the fingers of Baba there poured into her mouth a small quantity of water which He said was from the river Ganges. Subbamma then joined the ranks of the released!"[20]

On November 23, 1950, on the occasion of Sai Baba's 24th birthday, the temple-ashram complex of Prasanthi Nilayam was officially inaugurated. It was then a simple-looking building, with two stories built of granite. The central prayer hall, flanked by rooms on both sides, was the main part of the building. Now there was more space for spiritual seekers who came to see Sai Baba. They came to purify their souls by detaching from their normal everyday lives and joined other seekers in prayers and songs (bhajans). They hoped to achieve spiritual healing and maturity by following instructions from their guru, Sai Baba.

Soon Sai Baba realized that along with spiritual healing, the visitors as well as the people of Puttaparthi and neighboring villages needed physical healing. So, he built a hospital on the hills behind his residence, overlooking the Chitravati River. This was a rather small hospital; it contained six beds for male and six beds for female patients. It had equipment for maternity cases and a room with an x-ray unit. Baba thought people who came to the hospital for physical ills would naturally turn to Prasanthi Nilayam for the treatment of their spiritual ills, so the two buildings complemented each other.

The turning points of public recognition of Sai Baba's presence came in April 1967 at the First All-India Conference in Madras and at the First World Conference in Bombay in May, 1968, when he reached about 40 years of age. It is said that by 1971 he had more than 6 million followers, and that his work was carried forward by 1,500 nonprofit organizations set up throughout India, all of them accountable to his Central Trust.

In 1973 Sai Baba decided to expand the temple and give it a more religious appearance. The Poornachandra Auditorium, which seats 15,000 to 20,000 people, was built to hold the throngs of devotees who visited him. The ashram went through major changes, and it was gradually transformed into what it is today. A beautiful dome was erected atop the temple, which, along with other additions, gave a majestic and sacred appearance to the building. Many attractive sculptures of various Hindu gods were installed. Prasanthi Nilayam now contains a beautifully decorated mansion of more than 7,500 square feet, including huge prayer rooms, dining halls, and massive sculptures. The new additions were completed by November 23, 1974, when followers of Sai Baba celebrated his 48th birthday. N. Kasturi suggests that Sai Baba himself was the architect and engineer who directed the construction of building. Curious engineers and architects who visit the building are amazed by Sai Baba's sense of perspective and fine aesthetic vision.

As Baba became more popular in India and around the world, his ashram, Prasanthi Nilayam, became an internationally known pilgrimage center. Devotees came from all over the world, and there was clearly a need to build hotels, grocery stores, a post office, a police station, and other facilities to provide the ever-growing visitors as well as devotees who resided in the area with their necessities. To demonstrate his ecumenical mission, Sai Baba built a religious museum to commemorate the spiritual beliefs of various religious traditions. His museum contained models of diverse religious structures, including the Golden Temple of Amristar (the most sacred temple of the Sikhs, located in Amritsar), and the mosque of Mecca (the most sacred place for Muslims, now located in Saudi Arabia). The little village of Puttaparthi gradually increased to a massive size, turned into a prosperous town, and now receives visitors from all over the world. The divine little boy who entertained his classmates by materializing objects grew up to become an internationally known figure, one worshipped by influential people, including governors and even the Prime Minister of India. On his 43rd birthday on November 23, 1968, in a moving speech, Sai Baba announced his mission as the savior of humanity to all peoples of the world. (See Appendix.)

6

Avatar of the Age

Whenever righteousness diminishes and evil arises,
I sent myself forth.
To protect the good people and to destroy the evil ones
To establish righteousness, I incarnate myself age after age.

—Bhagavad Gita 4:7–8

To adherents of monotheistic religions, the concept of an avatar (or avatara) is not an easy one to comprehend, but in Hindu culture it is an age-old concept and a familiar aspect of Hinduism. In Hinduism, gods and goddesses intervene on behalf of human beings, and when needed they appear in human form. Brahma, the creator; Vishnu (Visnu), the preserver; and Shiva (Siva), the destroyer, are the three major gods of Hinduism. These are three manifestations of the supreme God that work together to manage the affairs of the universe. These three aspects of God are depicted as male, with each having female consorts (partners) in the highly complex iconography of India. Hindu religious imagery also ascribes animal-symbols to each of the three aspects and to their partners.

Followers of Hinduism see all of creation as an interplay among these three primary forces. Brahma is represented by a symbol and a sound, OM (Aum), which indicates the unchanging, universal, and supreme Godhead. According to Hindu teachings, by this sound-symbol, all that we know was created and all of life is sustained.[21] This sound (perhaps the same concept as the Big Bang of modern physics) is considered to contain all of the wisdom of the Vedas and other sacred scriptures of Hinduism, and it is widely chanted as a devotional and meditative practice.

Each practitioner of Hinduism has a personalized conception of the Deity, and these forms number in the hundreds of thousands. There are numerous local deities, and uncountable family deities or household gods. Thus, there are innumerable forms of devotional and spiritual practice, and the usual practitioner worships his or her cherished form in a ceremony called a *puja*. Pujas invariably include a ritual of purification, offerings, and prayers, which are performed in the spirit of *bhakti*, or devotion.

Although many people in India are illiterate, and few are familiar with sacred texts even in oral tradition, Hinduism does have sacred literature, and it falls into two broad categories. The first is that of the classical *Vedas*, said to be received by sages from Divinity; and the second is the *Upanishads* ("insights"), composed by illuminated and often unknown sages. Of the former, there are four, and they form the basis of Vedanta (the philosophy put forth by the Vedas). Of the latter, there are 108 currently in existence, although most attention is given to about ten. The Vedas describe codes of activity and what constitutes right knowledge, the duties and rights of humans, and the obligations and responsibilities of all stages of life. The *Upanishads* are so vast and varied that they defy brief description, but in general they are inspired wisdom-writings that are concerned with the perception of reality and the human's place within it.

Additional quasi-sacred texts include two *puranas* or epic texts, the *Ramayana*, or tales of *Rama*, and the *Mahabharata*, which includes the *Bhagavad Gita*, in which Krishna is the central figure. These clarify the Vedas, and their tales are meant to make clear spiritual truths. Much of India's popular religious culture is centered on tales of Rama and Krishna. In practice, a follower of the Hindu path adopts a *yoga* or path of unification with the Deity or the attainment of one's ideals. The two most widely followed yogas are *bhakti* yoga, or the devotional path, in which one worships or shows devotion to a divine figure or a spiritual guide, and *jnana* yoga, or the path of attaining knowledge through mental discipline and learning.

In Hinduism, one will easily find innumerable varieties of spiritual techniques that cover a wide spectrum of practice. These are too numerous to summarize here, but some are known in the West. These include chanting of sacred texts and songs, repetition of sacred phrases, exercise of postures and poses; also included are classical techniques of breathing exercises and repetition of sacred sounds (mantras), concentration, contemplation, meditation, study of sacred texts, and a variety of austere practices carried out by those who renounce the material world. Nothing is exempted from inclusion in religious practices and spiritual techniques, and it is not unusual to find specific sexual practices and diets incorporated into one's yoga.

By claiming personal sanctification and embodiment of divinity, Satya Sai Baba probably shocks most traditional practitioners of Western religions. In Islam, Christianity, and Judaism, to claim personal embodiment of God is considered blasphemy, the greatest of wrongdoings. By contrast, Hinduism insists upon the reality of *avatar*. This is a Sanskrit word that means "the descent of God" from Absolute Deity to a human or personal form of the Supreme Being. Furthermore, some trends within Hindu thought suggest that there are innumerable such divine forms that reside in an eternal spiritual realm that can manifest itself as needed.

The most widely accepted definition of *avatar* is found in the Chaitanya-charitamrita, dictated by the sage Chaitanya in Benares in 1528 to his disciple Sanatana Goswami, in which he states an avatar or incarnation of Godhead descends from the realm of God to manifest in material form and reveal itself to material creation. In the West, we commonly use the term "incarnation" to explain this idea, but this term is inherently misleading, as Hinduism does not think of an avatar as a divine soul or spirit entrapped in physical flesh, but a soul and body that are both of the same divine essence and are as such free from the usual laws of time, space, and matter that govern the human condition. Krishna and Rama are believed to be avatars.

In Hindu thought, such a being is of the highest order, and far beyond the states of sanctification attained by sages and gurus and other spiritual masters, whose function it is to dispel ignorance and cause wisdom and moral values to spontaneously arise in the hearts and minds of their devotees and followers. Those who believe in an avatar insist they are possessed of divine attributes, including omniscience, omnipresence, and omnipotence, as well as unconditional love and compassion. At that, Hindus also uphold that avatars may be fully or partially empowered.

The idea of avatars is one of the most important beliefs of Hinduism, insofar as Hinduism holds a widespread belief that when *dharma* ("right living") decays among humans, divinity manifests itself in human form to reestablish by teaching and example the right path in life. The other three most widespread beliefs within Hinduism are (1) the concept of rebirth (reincarnation) in a series of lives according to the merits one accrues by right behavior, (2) the concept of *karma* or that every act has its eventual consequence, and that the effects of these consequences is cumulative (the human soul or *jiva* is thus compelled to annul its debits and credits of karma to attain liberation from rebirth), and (3) the concept of a caste system, a religio-social structure that holds that every human is born into a place within society according to the merits accrued in previous lifetimes—indeed, that humans may be reborn into animal or insect forms because of insufficient or bad karma. This latter belief may be the religious encodement of ages-old attempts to construct and maintain order within society.

It is worth our attention that when Satya Sai Baba first announced he was an avatar, he claimed to be a reincarnation of Krishna, who is depicted as being from the lowest of all castes, a very dark-skinned cow herder from a remote rural village. Krishna himself is said to be an avatar and an incarnation of Vishnu. Thus, the simple statement of Satya Sai Baba placed him outside the caste system by reason of divinity—above all the masters, saints, and sages by reason of his incarnation of Godhead—and endeared him to the low-born and outcasts of the Indian social structure. Furthermore, he confounded religious experts by claiming to be a reincarnation of an incarnation.

The Satya Sai Baba organization official website has posted the transcriptions of four of Sai Baba's discourses that they have determined to be especially significant. Three of these discourses include his statements about being an avatar or personification of Deity. In the fourth, he discloses that he possesses divine abilities. In a discourse given on Guru Pournima Day, July 6, 1963, Sai Baba began a speech, then stopped, barely able to speak, asked for water, and began stroking his left leg with both hands, apparently to cure himself of a stroke that he had endured for eight days. He said he had taken on the stroke for one of his devotees, and that this was not the first time he had done such a thing.[22] In this discourse, he states that his previous incarnation in the form of Sai Baba of Shirdi was an incarnation of Shiva, that his current incarnation was of Shiva and *Shakthi* together, and that his future incarnation would be as Shakthi alone in the form of *Prema Sai.*[23]

In a discourse at the World Conference of Bhagawan Sri Satya Sai Organizations in Bombay, May 17, 1968, he stated plainly he is an incarnation of God and has come to restore righteousness. He stated that his followers "cannot understand the nature of my reality" and that "any moment my Divinity may be revealed to you" and they must "endeavor to overcome the *maya* (illusion) that hides it from your eyes." He further states:

SAI CHAKRA (YANTRA)

The *Sai Chakra* or *Yantra* (*yanthra*) is a mystic diagram composed of graphics of lines, circles, curves, and so on, that contains Sai Baba's divine seven-dimensional seed-principles. The purpose of the Sai Chakra is to enable his devotees to realize their highest Divine potential. The *Chakra* or *Yantra* maps out systematically the steps in the integral evolution of Sai spiritual consciousness. The Sacred Seed *Mantras* or formulae filling the diagram contain the essence of Sai Spirituality. The Sai Yantra contains an integral subtle picture of the Sai study of human awareness, theology, and customary practices to reach Divinity. That is why *Yantra* worship is considered superior to image worship, which is at a grosser level. Points of the *Yantra* correlate with the inner forces in each individual and link them with divine cosmic energies.

The contemplation of the Sai *Chakra* activates or turns our inner wheel (*Chakra*) of Spiritual energy to open vistas of Divine Truth, Goodness, and Beauty for realization of the eternal and universal principle of Divine Bliss (*Ananda*). The inner flowering of Sai consciousness results in the outer manifestation of pure love for all beings without distinction and of selfless service to needy and suffering humans. This is the fulfillment of a life leading to Self- and God-realization.

Source: *http://www.eaisai.com/baba/*.

This is a human form in which every divine entity, every divine principle, that is to say, all the names and forms ascribed by man to God, are manifest . . . you will be convinced that the basic reason for this . . . adoration of millions from all over the world . . . is this supra-worldly Divinity in human form.[24]

In a discourse given on his 43rd birthday in 1968, he spoke about being an avatar: "For the protection of the virtuous, for the destruction of evil-doers and for establishing righteousness on a firm footing, I incarnate from age to age."

In a discourse given June 9, 1974, he spoke on several issues:

1. God, Who is inscrutable and in the very heart of every being, and must be sought in the depths of ourselves.

2. The religion of love: "I am the embodiment of divine love, love is my instrument."

3. Other holy men, who fail to see who he is, and that it is he from whom the Vedas they study emanated for their sake. "What I will, must take place, what I plan, must succeed, I am Truth, and Truth has no need to hesitate, or fear, or bend."

4. Why he materializes gifts: he regards this as trivial and the least of what he can offer, and that he pities those who "allow themselves so easily to lose precious awareness of My Divinity." He gives these things to "signalize the bond between me and those to whom they are given . . . love is the bond that wins grace."

5. What the name Sai Baba means, a pun on *Sa* = "divine," *ai* or *ayi* = "Mother," and *Baba* = "Father," thus, he is a source of unselfish parental-like love, who has come to unite all of humanity as one family.[25]

To some, Satya Sai Baba is divine, an avatar, God Himself, or at least a guru of sufficiently high attainment that he is able to defy what we think we know about the laws of nature. Naturally, he has his detractors also, the most extreme of whom decry him as a magician or opportunist at best, and as a criminal or demon at worst. Accusations and allegations of serious wrongdoing can readily be found in the press and on Websites, mixed among the accounts of his teachings and of his service to humanity, and they are widespread and well known.

It is not within the scope of this small book to discuss accusations and determine if they are true or not. It would be more useful to acknowledge that such situations are not unusual, and to discuss in general how a devotee or follower can approach such a situation should it become an immediate reality. At the least, it may be helpful to discuss the usual dynamics of what happens when a beloved spiritual figure is accused of wrongdoing.

The dilemma is a classic one. If serious allegations are ignored, those who do not pursue the truth participate in what may be a cover-up, and more persons may be harmed, thus a devotee has a moral obligation to investigate, inform, and act accordingly. If serious allegations are publicized without critical thinking and investigation, we may contribute to the spread of untruth. There are always ramifications. One is that if allegations are untrue, one has contributed to defamation and hindered the worthwhile work of another. Another is that if they prove to be true, and the investigator does not contribute to a correction of wrongdoing, the situation in which wrongdoing happens may be strengthened, and the wrongdoing may be amplified. To start at the very beginning, one would have to raise a question about why anyone would look outside him- or herself to seek guidance in personal transformation. A general answer would be twofold.

The first part of the answer is that we are not capable of being objective about ourselves, and we have blind spots about our motivations and behaviors. These can only be addressed by another person, one who is compassionate and insightful, someone who has no investment in maintaining an illusion or misperception about ourselves as we so often do, and this role is usually fulfilled by a religious figure, psychological expert, or close and trusted friend.

The other part is that spiritual and religious transformation, or at least the remaking of our personality, is always accompanied by a redefinition of our role in the world, thus our process is never completely individual, but has a social aspect as well. Isolation is detrimental to transformation, except for periods of retreat, when they are appropriate. It is largely for support of transformation and growth and change that religious communities and congregations form, and additional reasons include banding together from kinship in a belief system, mutual support in the face of an indifferent or hostile society, and an intention to combine resources to attain goals.

The key elements that bind a devotee to a teacher-figure, and that bind a group of practitioners or devotees to each other, are mutual good will and trust. When this trust is betrayed, or when there is a perception or even a misperception that this trust has been betrayed, the devotee will be left devastated.

To this basic twofold concept, one can add the specific cases of religions or wisdom-ways in which spiritual attainment is the direct result not of meritorious actions and sincere practice, but of being under the umbrella of grace conveyed by a sanctified human personage. Many gurus and sanctified persons (including Sai Baba) teach their followers that it is only by remaining in their favor that their followers, devotees, and supporters can transcend their mundane, meaningless lives.

In the European-American West, we tend to be cynical about public figures in general and about religious and spiritual teachers in particular, and we tend to be suspicious about anyone who claims to have attained an elevated state of existence. This perspective is in basic conflict with our knowledge that human improvement and moral and ethical advancement are realities. In fact, a healthy person deeply desires to heal and transcend his or her perceived shortcomings. The roots of our cynicism and suspicion are in the knowledge that others face the same inner struggles we face, and are prey to the same faults and temptations to which we may succumb, thus, when they fail, we question our inner struggle toward transformation also.

It certainly can neither be proven nor disproved that Sai Baba is an embodiment of Divinity and an avatar, neither more nor less than the existence of God can be proven or disproved. The Supreme Being, however one conceives of such a thing, is by definition transcendent of all human intellectual activity, including any process by which "proof" could be established. In religious and spiritual matters, practitioners are usually trained to integrate their intellectual and rational capacities into an overall personality that acknowledges something as transcendental and sublime, and "proof" lies within the practitioner in the way his or her personality is reshaped and his or her moral and ethical qualities are elevated as a result of increased insight into Divine nature and into his or her own human nature.

One can make what one will of the claims of Sai Baba. His followers are not forced to accept and profess that he is God. Not all of his devotees accept that he is the embodiment of absolute Divinity, and many accept him as a guru or a primary personal source of guidance for their spiritual transformation and fulfillment of social purpose. Although in the European-American West, those who claim divinity are viewed as blasphemers, eccentrics, or mentally unstable, such claims are viewed as a real possibility within Hindu cultures, and a believer's sense of frustration and anger is vastly amplified when a proclaimed avatar is accused of wrongdoing.

On one hand, God is the Supreme Being, and to make any accusation against an omniscient God, whose ways are unfathomable to a mere human, is an extreme outrage and a sign one is not a devotee or follower at all. When challenged, people of such a mental and emotional makeup tend to "entrench" further into their conceptions and belief system. On the other hand, the disenchantment or disappointment of followers who feel betrayed may be genuine and rooted in reality. It is worth our while to explore first the nature of the relationship between a spiritual guide and his or her followers, which could be called a "guide and guided" relationship.

We may well wonder what the daily life of such a person is like. Can we gain any insight into such a being by how they move through the world of humans? We are fortunate to have the eyewitness accounts of Schulman, recorded in 1971, which the followers of Sai Baba say he still generally follows, although Sai Baba is, at time of this writing, almost 79 years old.

Schulman recorded that in Prasanthi Nilayam ashram, Baba would rise and bathe at 6:00 A.M., then present himself to his devotees at 6:30 A.M., and then drink coffee or tea and hold discussions with selected followers afterward for a half-hour. At 7:00 A.M. he walks through a gathering of his devotees who have gathered in the pre-dawn darkness, some of whom attempt to hand him written petitions, and he selects some for private interviews. The deliberate act of allowing oneself to be seen by devotees is called *darshan*, literally "seeing," and is said to convey blessings by mere presence and not because of any personal interaction.

Many of his followers report that the simple sight of Baba has an extraordinary effect upon them. At 9:30 A.M. he returns to a dining room for breakfast, and then meets with foreigners and celebrities from 10:00 to 11:00 A.M. There is *bhajan* singing afterward, followed by more private interviews, after which Baba reviews mail from 12:00 noon to 1:00 P.M., reviews business matters, and then rests from 2:30 to 3:00 P.M. He arises again, and again has coffee or tea and discussion with followers. Because of a significant increase in the number of visitors, Sai Baba now holds another darshan around 4:00 P.M. The afternoon darshan is followed by more private interviews until 6:30 P.M., then he inspects projects around his ashram until the time for more bhajan singing, until 7:30 P.M. He then supervises meditation until dinner at 8:00 P.M. He gives attention to other work until midnight. He then rests.

His devotees say he sleeps very little, and that he instead enters into a deep trance state, during which he may talk, and usually moves his right arm and hand around. When asked about this, Baba said that his arm movements have to do with assistance to beings at a distance or in the unseen realms of existence. Satya Sai Baba travels throughout India, including visits to his projects and other ashrams, but apparently he rarely makes his plans known in advance, and only to a very small circle of supporters. He has been known to leave spontaneously and without any advance notice. When he travels, he takes advantage of the comfort of modern luxury automobiles, and he is heavily guarded. Given the discomfort and vagaries of the Indian rail system, and the reality that there are deranged persons who roam the world who wish to harm those who are well known, this is understandable.

7

Teachings and Followers

I am new and ever ancient. I come always for the restoration of Dharma (righteousness), for tending the virtuous and ensuring them conditions congenial for progress, and for educating the "blind" who miss the way and wander into the wilderness. Some doubters might ask, can Parabrahman assume human form? Well, man can derive joy only through the human frame; he can receive instruction, inspiration, illumination only through human language and human communication.

—Satya Sai Baba

Those who believe that religion and spirituality have some basis in reality often hold certain belief systems, which can provide them with prescribed ethical and moral codes of conduct and that to some extent explain the human connection with the divine. Following prescribed ethical and moral codes of conduct, they believe, will elevate human harmony and ease human suffering. Through spiritual beliefs, they hope to improve their inner strength of character, so they can counter the harsh effects of everyday life. Such people often shape their behavior according to the teachings of an ideal or exemplar. These spiritual gurus, sages, saints, and ascended masters have been around for most of human history.

Although some of these sages have reached enlightenment unaided, most sincere spiritual seekers tend to follow in the footsteps of those who have achieved "enlightenment." Enlightened masters often possess deep insights into the nature of their sincere devotees and thus can help them on their path to find the immense treasure of enlightenment that is within their reach. The guru points out the path, warns them about the dangers and pitfalls, offers them encouragement, and clarifies methods of advancement.

Sai Baba is a spiritual guru who has attracted millions of spiritual seekers to himself, some of whom consider him to be an avatar. The sincere devotees of Sai Baba believe that the boundary between human and Divine has been erased in the person of Sai Baba, and he is truly a living God who can be followed as an ideal model of righteous life. In Sai Baba they have found their ideal divine being, the one who can be their savior as well as ultimate teacher. Through him they hope to go through spiritual transformations that are beyond the domain of neurology, physics, and psychology.

His followers come from all walks of life. Sai Baba does not require that anyone who approaches him and his teachings be a believer from the beginning. He is not offering his followers any new religion. Actually, he insists that those who come to him continue to follow the religion they have been following in their lives, and he does not require that they adopt him as their ideal of attainment. Naturally, those who are attracted to him do adopt him in this capacity to varying degrees, and some even believe that he is the embodiment of the Divine and revere and worship him on a level that followers of monotheistic religions reserve for God alone.

Devotees believe that their spiritual transformation is directed by Sai Baba's grace and intervention. To them Sai Baba is a deity possessing an indescribable force. They seek attainment of spiritual fulfillment through devotion and service (*bhakti yoga*), the path of unselfish action (*karma yoga*), or study and practice (*jnana yoga*), which are the three primary approaches to religion in Hinduism. In Sai Baba, they have found another human who has attained a state deemed transcendent of normal human limitation. Where either devotional or knowledge-seeking behavior is used for spiritual enlightenment, such activity is often focused on a human perceived as an ideal model. This activity may be simply continuous study of teachings given in written or oral form, or one may undertake a rigorous discipline of exercises and practices that are recommended by a teacher-figure, and one may also choose to participate in the work of a teacher-figure by giving support in the form of financial assets or actual labor to his or her goals, as many of Sai Baba's followers do.

Satya Sai Baba attracts all kinds of seekers, including cynics and skeptics, the curious, followers, disciples, and supporters. He recommends they all adopt his primary essential teaching that has become his motto: "Love all, serve all." He wants his followers to uphold his Four Principles:

1. There is only one religion, the religion of love.

2. There is only one language, the language of the heart.

3. There is only one race, the race of humanity.

4. There is only one God, and He is omnipresent.

He asks his followers to enact his Nine-point Code of Conduct:

1. Daily meditation and prayer.

2. Group devotional singing or prayer with family members once a week.

3. Participation in Sai Spiritual Education by children of the family.

4. Participation in community service work and other programs of the organization.

5. Regular attendance at the Center's devotional meetings.

6. Regular study of Satya Sai Baba literature.

7. Not speaking ill of others, especially in their absence.

8. Practice placing a ceiling on desires—consciously and continually.

9. Striving to eliminate the tendency to waste time, money, food, and energy—and utilizing the savings for service to mankind.

He also asks that they follow his Tenfold Path to Divinity:

1. Love and serve the Motherland; do not hate or hurt the motherlands of others.

2. Honor every religion; each is a pathway to the one God.

3. Love all men without distinction; know that mankind is a single community.

4. Keep your home and its environs clean; it will ensure health and happiness for you and society.

5. Do not throw coins when beggars stretch their hands for alms; help them to become self-reliant. Likewise, provide food and shelter, and love and care, for the sick and aged.

6. Do not tempt others by offering bribes or demean yourself by accepting bribes.

7. Do not harbor jealousy, hatred, or envy on any count.

8. Do not depend on others to serve your personal needs,
but become your own servant before proceeding to serve
others.

9. Observe the laws of the state and be an exemplary citizen.

10. Adore God; abhor sin. [For a more detailed explanation of
Sai Baba's Tenfold Path to Divinity, see Appendix.]

Finally, he asks that followers support his Threefold Objectives:

1. Free education, primary to post-graduate level.

2. Free medical treatment for all.

3. Free treatment for purification and a constant supply of
drinking water. [26]

His followers are encouraged to devote as much time and
effort to their inner connection upon him as they are inclined
to. Through his writings and discourses, his followers are
provided with many avenues of devotional activities, which
include prayer, singing, and meditation. [27] Some of his recommended practices are widely used by his followers throughout
the world.

The first practice that Sai Baba recommends is that his followers greet each other in a real meeting of souls, by using spiritual
terms such as "*Sai Ram*," "*OM*," "*Hari OM*," or some other
sacred expression, and not to follow that with senseless chatter.
The word *Sai* when split into *Sa* and *Ai* means "universal father"
(Sa) and "universal mother" (Ai), so Sai is the divinity who
serves as our mother and father. *Ram* is short for *Rama*,
meaning "God"; it also could mean the destruction of illusion. [28]
OM or *Aum* is the divine sound and *Hari OM* means "O God";

it is often used to call Vishnu, the Hindu God of sustenance. Fundamentally, Sai Baba wishes his followers to purposefully greet each other as manifestations of Divinity, and perhaps to witness and remind each other of divinity in each other, instead of seeing each other as random collisions of personalities.

Second, Sai Baba places great emphasis on a sequence of sacred phrases called a *mantra*, especially one called the *Gayatri* mantra. This mantra can be interpreted to mean the following:

SPIRITUAL DEVELOPMENT & DEVOTION TO GOD
Selected from Sai Baba's Discourses

Let every human being remake himself. Let us understand that we live not for money making, not for fulfilling our wants, not for scholarly and intellectual pursuits, but for spiritual development. Effects of Karmas of the past have to be effaced with Karmas backed by Love (*Prema*). Every Karma must have a background of love. It is only in this world that spiritual progress can be made. Annihilation of the ego and dissolution of desires can be made here and now. Conquer desires, the little "I" feeling. Fill the heart with the Light of *Prema* so that the evil qualities of hate, greed and conceit find no place therein. In winnowing, the dry outer coverings are separated from the grain. So too, you should separate the bad thoughts and emotions from the good and healthy ones. (Spiritual purity can be achieved through sincere devotion to God.)

The object of devotion should be to realize God in your heart and allow Him to fill all parts of your being with His light and power. This done, your hearts will be overflowing with Divine Love towards all beings in the world. Your eyes will see only God everywhere. Your hands will work only for the good of everybody and you will ultimately become the very embodiments of God, filled with bliss and ever surcharged with ecstasy.

In this state, the difference between the *Bhakta* and *Bhagavan* will disappear. The *Bhakta* by constant remembrance and surrender to God becomes God Himself. So when you constantly think of God, you become His very image. Then it is you that enjoys immortal joy and peace.

We contemplate the glory of Light illuminating the three worlds: gross, subtle, and causal;

I am that life-giving power, love, radiant illumination, and divine grace of universal intelligence;

We pray for the divine light to illumine our minds.

The first line depicts the unity of body, mind, and soul. The second line affirms the devotee's capacity to dispel the darkness of his or her ignorance. The third line means that the overwhelming radiance of the Divine reality is the sole agent of the devotee's transformation. When recited in the original Sanskrit with the correct accents, the audio power of this mantra is quite striking and amplifies its psychological impact. Sai Baba has taught that this mantra is a mother-like sustaining force that animates all life and requests his followers not to neglect repeating it. He has also called this mantra the *Veda Sara*, or essence of the four Vedas or sacred texts. Veda literally means "knowledge," and this mantra is believed to increase and sharpen the follower's faculty of knowledge. The mantra is sacred because it demonstrates the fundamental principle of spiritual endeavor: that a sublime Unity underlies the countless forms that embody creation. It is the goal of the seeker to recognize this Unity, and thus understand the interplay of a seemingly endless multiplicity of forms. Our innermost self or *atma*, not our provisional identity, is identical with this Unity.[29]

Sai Baba's teachings embody three aspects of devotion: praise, meditation, and prayer. That is to say, although devotees may feel they do not experience Divinity, they praise the Supreme Being anyway, because according to Sai Baba, praise is due to Divinity, and all must give their deepest consideration to the all-pervading Presence of Divinity through meditation. Sai Baba teaches that all must admit the limitations of their wisdom and what they consider knowledge and to pray for the strengthening of their minds and the ability to discriminate, so they will be able to perceive reality as it is and not as they wish it to be. Meditation is useful and effective only when minds are stable and turned toward God, however God is conceived. To attain this mental stability and direction, one must meditate and pray regularly, which also affirms the validity of the experiences that arises from meditation and prayer.

Sai Baba recommends that his followers recite the term *shanti* ("peace") three times as a benediction at the end of their prayers, singing (*bhajans*), or chanting mantras—once each for body, mind, and soul. The word *shanti* is usually repeated three times, preceded by *OM* (i.e., *OM shanti, shanti, shanti-hi*). He recommends that his followers recite the Gayatri mantra in the morning, at noon, and in the evening, the three times that are called the *sandhya kalam,* or times of union. He teaches that doing so will reduce the effects of wrong actions committed during the course of the day. Sai Baba says these times will implant the mantra in our daily cycle of *sattva* (balance, peace, and pure serenity, in early morning and evening), *rajas* (emotion, passion, restlessness, and our activities of daily duties from morning through late afternoon), and *tamas* (our inertia, ignorance, inaction, and repose during our nocturnal period.) He recommends that his followers recite it instead of singing popular songs; he affirms that reciting it when we bathe will also cleanse our mind and intellect, and that we should also recite it before each meal, when we awake, and before we go to sleep.

Sai Baba ascribes several benefits of the regular recitation of mantras. These include the following:

1. Protection of our bodies, and improvement of our intellects and our power of speech

2. The descent of Divine splendor, which will illuminate our intellect and clarify our path

3. Relief from diseases

4. Warding off misery

5. Fulfillment of our deepest desires

6. The emergence of various kinds of powers in our lives

7. The emergence of a growing attitude of surrender toward the Divine

8. The bestowal of all that is beneficial

9. The supplanting of evil tendencies with virtuous habits, and the acquisition of Divine powers (or *Devashakti*)

The third practice that Sai Baba recommends is the recitation of two passages of the *Bhagavad Gita* (chapter 4, verse 24, and chapter 15, verse 14):

> The act of offering is God,
> The oblation is God,
> By God it is offered to the fire of God,
> God is That which is to be attained
> By the one who sees God in all,

and,

> Becoming the life-fire in the bodies of all living things,
> Mingling with the upward and downward breaths
> (a reference to the currents of life energy within the human),
> I digest the four kinds of foods.

Fourth, Sai Baba emphasizes the power of prayers and meditations. He differentiates the two from each other, however. Prayer, he notes, is the activity of the supplicant, who surrenders to Divinity, whereas meditation tends to bring divinity and humanity together, with neither on a higher or lower level. He is clear about meditation being something that emerges from within us, and as such it cannot be taught, other than the techniques and practices, such as postures and positions, breathing, and so on. Sai Baba has repeated to his followers the advice of the great sage Ramana Maharshi not to pay attention to a specific amount of time that should be devoted to daily meditation. Instead, Ramana Maharshi taught that one should continue until one forgets that one is trying to meditate, because if we are aware of our effort, we are not meditating at all—we are enmeshed in self-thought instead of experiencing the presence of Divinity.

Paradoxically, he insists that a spiritual practitioner does not need to rely on the influence of a sage or yogi or master to succeed in meditation and instead recommends repetition of a name of God (*japa yoga* or *namasmarana*) and inward prayer toward God. Nonetheless, in awareness of his own mission, and of the difference between those who are able to be in his presence regularly and those who must learn from afar, he has made certain that his own discourses are recorded and published for purposes of guidance. He teaches that regular practice is the surest method to become successful at meditation and recommends the early morning hours, between 3:00 A.M. and 6:00 A.M., and also the evening, after dusk, as the best times. In terms of technique, he advises it is beneficial to hold a constant gaze upon a flame, worship-figure, or an inspiring picture for 12 seconds at a time without blinking, to develop one's concentration (*dharana*). Concentration is an essential primary skill that any spiritual seeker should develop; without it, one cannot focus one's attention and attain stillness, and both are required for meditation.

In addition to practicing concentration and meditation, he recommends sitting comfortably upon a mat or cushion, to mark a separation between the Earth and the practitioner, and sitting as straight as is possible. The hands should be relaxed in the lap, one palm on another with the thumb-tips touching, or the wrists can rest upon the knees with the palms of the hands facing upward, thumb-tips touching forefinger-tips and the other fingers spread out (*chin mudra*). The tongue is stilled by resting the tongue-tip on the rear of the front teeth. Meditation is of a higher order, in that there is neither object nor subject to be contemplated, and our thoughts are stilled and our senses are transcended.[30]

As a fifth practice, Satya Sai Baba ascribes enormous effectiveness to the right use of words, especially to divine names or attributes. He teaches that the best use of the tongue, of our capacity for speech, is to dwell on any divine name, and that we should make every effort to restrain from thoughtless speech and its harmful effects. He has quoted the sage Vyasa, who said that we are most fortunate to be born in this age, called the *kali yoga*, in which it is much easier to earn the grace of Divinity by repetition of the names of divinity, instead of carrying out rigorous self-denial and penance, as was required in past ages for attainment of spiritual enlightenment or liberation.

In truth, we carry around most of our memories and mental agitation and activity in the form of words, and we barely think about the contents of our thoughts. Even basic Western psychology tells us that we may think of ourselves in visual forms and images, but we especially define ourselves in terms of the impact words have had upon us throughout our lives. It follows that words have a tremendous significance regarding our transformation to an enlightened state.

Mystics in all places and times have paid close attention to the impact of different kinds of sounds upon our condition. Sai Baba teaches that a seeker may invoke Divinity by any of thousands of names, and that if we repeat any one of them with love and faith, doing so will bring divine grace upon us. His teachings on the benefits of reciting divine names (called *smarana* in Sanskri, and *dhikr* in the Sufi path) cover several points.

Repeating divine names is the best antidote for all illnesses. It is like a boat that conveys us across the ocean of birth and death. It is a source of consolation, courage, and a realistic perspective. It is the most effective discipline for our age. It will give us all the results found by means of any other practice. It is a fountain of energy. It will protect us throughout life. It is the best of inner activities. It keeps our mental activities under control. It gives us a feeling of nearness to God.

By invoking Deity, Sai Baba teaches, the effects of previous births (*prarabdha*) are nullified. Calling divine names is reliable to erase the troubles of a journey. It is the source of all consciousness. It erases the effects of wrongdoing powerfully and effectively. It is an excellent way to counter delusion. It helps the mind to withdraw from being enmeshed in the senses.[31]

Satya Sai Baba says that one may repeat a chosen name spontaneously and creatively, by associating it with a form, by using other names connected with it, by paying attention to its sound, and by associating it with other pleasant sensations and memories. He also recommends use of a string of counting-beads, called a *japa mala* in Hinduism, which takes us to the practice of chanting the 108 *Namavali* or names of the Lord.[32]

The practice of the invocation of 108 Names of the Lord (Namavali), often counted on a garland of 108 beads, is the sixth practice widely used by followers of Satya Sai Baba.[33] Each name is preceded by the primal sound "*OM,*" and then usually the word *Sri,* meaning, approximately, "glory be to," and it is followed with the word *namah,* meaning "salutation." *Namah* itself is derived from two syllables, which together mean "no delusion," and thus signifies surrender of the conceptions of our ego. The name itself can be a characteristic, aspect, event-depiction, or some other reference to Divinity. The right approach to such repetition is difficult to tell solely from the published discourses of Sai Baba. On one hand, he recommends an attitude of sincere yearning to which divinity can respond, and on the other he teaches that one must worship without any desire whatsoever because God alone knows our deepest needs and we should thus remain detached from what we think we need. The number 108 is considered sacred for several reasons: One is that we breathe 200 sets of 108 breaths daily, another is that each digit adds up to nine, which has long been a sacred number in Asia (it is the cube of three, the number of orifices in the human body, and Satya Sai Baba teaches that this number represents Brahma). The number 108 is also the multiple of 9 times 12, another number deemed to have sacred significance.

The seventh practice Satya Sai Baba recommends for this followers is a recitation of group of three mantras. The eighth practice is adapted from an ages-old Hindu practice and involves concentration on a *yantra* or *chakra,* a complex symbolic geometrical diagram. The ninth and final practice is utilization of a seven-fold *tantra,* which is a mode of worship or spiritual technique, in some cases a ritual, for spiritual progress. There are verses associated with the first three steps. In essence, these constitute a *puja*, or ceremony, for contemplation and worship of Satya Sai Baba.

8

Love All, Serve All: Humanitarian Works

*Education without character,
science without humanity,
politics without principles and
commerce without morality
are not only useless, but positively dangerous.*

—Satya Sai Baba

One's values, Sai Baba notes, should be aligned with his or her thoughts, words, and deeds. A good devotee is one whose character is based on integrity, as displayed by his or her life, which should be devoted to peace, truth, love, right conduct, and nonviolence. A devotee with right conduct (*dharma*) would please his guru by serving humanity through good work. A devotee needs to recognize that he is a social being and therefore has obligations to society. His spiritual development will not be on the right path unless he has a humanitarian motivation.

According to Sai Baba, pure love, peace, truth, and humanitarian service please God more than anything else. One should not change religions to please God; one should become a better person by living life with integrity. To stand beside his words, Sai Baba has become involved in numerous charitable works. He believes that helping those in need is the best way to convince his followers that charitable works are divine acts. His devotees look up to him as their role model, so he hopes that they will also follow his path of humanitarianism. Sai Baba reminds his devotees that being righteous is serving humanity, and serving humanity is serving God: "If God Himself is here to foster *Dharma* (righteousness), and you engage yourself in the same task, then you are worshiping Him. Then you are near and dear to Him, for you are serving Him, His devotees, and yourself."

Sai Baba's motto of "Love all, serve all" is evident in his humanitarian work, which at this time has far-reaching importance. In the early 1970s, Sai Baba founded the "Sri Satya Sai Central Trust" as an umbrella organization for the supervision and management of the resources of his charitable work. The offices of this trust are located in Prasanthi Nilayam, his main residence in Puttaparthi. Today, after three decades, the work of the Trust is so widespread that it is difficult to construct an accurate accounting of its effectiveness. This expansiveness is the direct result of the supportive attitude and high esteem enthusiastically demonstrated by the followers of Sai Baba toward his humanitarian mission. It seems that many of his followers respond to their guru's advice to offer their talents for the good of humanity: "Whatever talent a person has should be dedicated to the rest of humanity indeed to all living beings. Therein lies fulfillment. Service to man will help your divinity to blossom, for it will gladden your heart and make you feel that life has been worth while. Service to man is service to God, for He is in every man, and every living being, in every stone and stump. Offer your talents at the feet of God."

Sai Baba's humanitarian work can be loosely divided into four categories that address educational development, health issues, relief to the rural impoverished, and public utility projects, especially in the field of water resources development.

EDUCATIONAL DEVELOPMENT

In 1981, Sai Baba founded an Institute of Higher Learning under his name that upholds not only high standards of academic excellence but also aims to develop high moral and ethical standards in its students. In a discourse on July 25, 1975, he clearly stated, "Spiritual education is not a separate and distinct discipline, but is part and parcel of all types and all levels of education."[34] Sai Baba spoke of his ideal, that "In this university, spiritual education will be integrated with ethical, physical, and metaphysical sciences." Remarkably, there is no charge for tuition, and only a very low fee, if any, for room and board. There are many Sai Baba Institutes around the world, built by his followers and modeled after the original Institute of Higher Learning. These are not directly controlled by the Central Trust, but are under the control of Sai Baba organizations within each country.

Given the emphasis on devotional singing at his ashrams and within the circles of his devotees, it is not surprising that Sai Baba also founded a music institute. The Sri Sathya Sai Institute of Music was founded in Puttaparthi around 2000; it contains a small music museum. Sai Baba and his followers have also founded several high schools and elementary schools.

Within the context of his Sai Organization, education is considered a "wing" on an equal level with devotion and service. He and his followers sometimes refer to this wing as "education in human values." These central values are taught as realization of divine love, truth and peace, actualization of one's duty, and maintaining a spirit of nonviolence if challenged. His institutes and schools have an Accreditation Commission that convenes regularly, on an international basis as well as at local and regional levels, and their proceedings are periodically made available in published form or on the Internet.

HEALTH ISSUES

India is a nation of extreme contrasts. It is a land that over the centuries has produced not only spiritual masters and philosophers of the highest nature, but also some of the most sophisticated mathematicians, logicians, engineers, scientists, agronomists, and the like, of all of Asia. At the same time, much of the population still lives in what is called Third World, but may be better described as premodern, conditions. The economy is mainly rural and agrarian for the majority of India's more than one billion people. These depend on the availability of water and access to land, and they are at the mercy of seasonal rains (monsoons) and other whims of climate. A significant portion of the country still does not have access to a steady supply of water, paved roads, modern transportation, and new techniques of farming. Other amenities such as electrical utilities, and modern communication media such as radio, television, telephones, and computers, are in short supply.

Whereas in developed parts of the world people often take for granted the fact that they have ready access to clean water, a safe food supply, and on-demand medicine and medical care, in many other parts of the developing world, such as portions of rural India, the level of poverty and underdevelopment is disheartening to outside visitors. In rural India, one of the greatest problems is the low availability of healthcare services and education, and this is compounded by extreme poverty, superstition, and a general lack of knowledge among the impoverished population of even the rudiments of hygiene. Thus, the Central Trust took upon itself the immense task of

HUMAN VALUES
Selected from Sai Baba's Discourses

What is the main reason for the well-being of the society? Our actions are the very cause. What is the reason for our actions? Actions result from our thoughts. What is the reason for action? The mind. What is the cause of the mind? Thought is the cause of the mind. If the thoughts are pure, the country will also become pure. We have to inculcate ideas, which are pure and good. These are human values.

What are these values? These are "Truth (*sathya*), Right Action (*dharma*), Peace (*shanti*), Love (*prema*) and Non-violence (*ahimsa*)." These five human values should be deemed as the fivefold life breaths. Since the values constitute the life breath, one who does not radiate the values in his actions is deemed to be lifeless!

What is this truth? Those words, which you speak with love, are truth. That which comes from the heart filled with love is truth. All that you do from a heart filled with love is *dharma*—righteousness. The heart, which is full of love in whatever it thinks, is peace. Then whatever actions you do with a heart filled with love is *ahimsa*—non-violence. So love is the foundation for all these. There is no life whatsoever without love. So one has to foster this love.

When the impulses arising from the heart are expressed in words, that is Truth (*sathya*). To put into action your words is Right Action (*dharma*). For all these Love is primary. Love in action is righteousness. Love in speech is truth. Love in thought is peace. Love in understanding is non-violence. When you realize that God is in everyone, you will practice non-violence.

Truth is man's nature; to be untrue is to be false to one's nature. *Dharma* is the practical application in real life of the ideal of Truth. *Shanthi* is the result of *Dharma* and *Prema* is the effulgence of *Shanthi*. Truth in words and truth and love in the heart is *Dharma*. *Prema* is the manner of speaking; Truth is the substance; *Dharma* is the language; *Santhi* is the result aimed at.

providing not only healthcare services, but also the founding of several institutions for the education of healthcare practitioners at all levels. As in all aspects of the work of Sai Baba, the basic teaching of "Love all, serve all" prevails, and in the domain of health care and education this basic teaching has been elaborated into four principles.

The first principle is that medical assistance is the right of every individual, regardless of his or her caste, religious beliefs, nationality, or skin color. This is a truly revolutionary principle, given the ages-old traditions in India. In the United States and Europe, the simple activity of a blood donation drive is taken for granted, whereas in India, blood donation drives raise profound issues that are related directly to racism, religious bigotry, hypernationalism, and the caste system. To surmount these issues at all is in itself an extraordinary achievement.

The second principle is that medical assistance and health care must be kept free from the overpowering influence of commercial interests. In some contrast to, for example, the United States, where there are several tiers of health care available depending upon one's economic resources, the Sai Baba organization upholds a belief that health is a basic right, and not a commodity or product to be bought, sold, or withheld according to market forces. Sai Baba did not set out to replicate in India in the name of modernization a Western-style system of health care provision with all its intricate and complicated entanglements of insurance companies, governmental and juridical interests, pharmaceutical and high-technology-equipment providers, and so on. His goal was simply to establish an organization of educated and skilled individuals who are dedicated to selfless service, and to the principle that free health care should be available to as many people as possible.

The third principle is a high level of emphasis upon the value of ethical personal interaction between workers who provide health care at all levels, and those who benefit from that care. In the view of Sai Baba and his followers, to be sick and dependent should not result in any loss of dignity, and the ill should expect to be treated according to the usual standards of medical practice, and also to be treated in a context that demonstrates five basic human values in every aspect of their care. These values are truth, righteousness, peace, love, and nonviolence.

The fourth principle is that spiritual well-being is valued as a medical concept. In the European-American West, strengthening the spirits and souls of the ill is either not upheld as an essential aspect of health care; or it is somewhat addressed on a doctrinal and pastoral level by those hospitals and clinics that are operated by formal religions; or, finally, it is relegated to the domain of psychotherapy and counseling. The followers of Sai Baba are trained to see patients as complex embodiments of a divine force that sustains all physical, psychological, and mental processes. Health care is delivered almost nationwide by a network of State Trusts that are guided by the Central Trust. Healthcare workers are expected to participate in many projects, including polio vaccination, blood donation, screening for eye diseases, and visiting hospitals and Hansen's disease (leprosy) enclaves.

Healthcare services are provided through a tri-level system, although the definitions used do not correspond to European-American conceptions of health care provision. Primary health care is provided at the most basic level by workers in the Sri Sathya Sai Seva (service) Organizations. These organizations send teams to remote rural areas to provide medicine free of cost through dispensaries, and especially to provide treatment of the many eye diseases that are prevalent throughout India by means of medicine and surgery, especially cataract surgery. Medical teams are also sent to orphanages, homes for abandoned elders, and Hansen's disease enclaves.

Secondary health care is provided in general hospitals. Currently, these are established at Puttaparthi, near Prasanthi Nilayam, and Whitefield, in Bangalore. Again, there is no charge to the patient for medical assistance. The hospitals are remarkably up-to-date in terms of their facilities and equipment. Both hospitals maintain specialized departments. The hospital at

Puttaparthi has units for medicine, pediatrics, orthopedic surgery, general surgery, urology, plastic surgery, ophthalmology (they maintain an eye tissue bank), gynecology and obstetrics, and ear-nose-throat surgery. The Sri Sathya Sai Institute of Higher Medical Sciences in Bangalore specializes in cardiac and neurological disorders only.

A third level of health care is provided at "super specialty" hospitals. These are smaller, specialized hospitals that provide, again free of charge, such services as cardiovascular surgery. The Sri Sathya Sai Institute of Higher Medical Sciences was opened on November 22, 1991, in Prasanthi Gram, which is about nine kilometers from the ashram, and near the small Sai Baba Airport. In a discourse prior to the opening of the Institute, Sai Baba recognized that few are interested in the healthcare needs of the poor, whether they live in rural or urban areas, and stated that the purpose of the Institute would be to provide services to the poor at no cost to them. The services provided are impressive and include cardiac procedures such as bypasses, respiratory system surgeries, kidney transplants, eye surgeries, and so on.

Naturally, given the immense task this Institute has taken upon itself in the face of the huge health problems of rural south India, there is usually a waiting list. In keeping with the principle of fair access to healthcare services, the admissions procedure includes a preliminary examination of a potential patient and a review of his or her overall situation; then, the type of assistance is decided by the Institute's committee. Calculation of need is supported by computer analysis of the data obtained about the patient to ensure impartiality. The Bangalore admissions procedure is similar to the facility at Puttaparthi. After a review of the patient's medical records, an appointment is made for evaluation, consultation, and possible registration and admission.

Because services are not paid for by insurance funds or money from their patients, this health care system depends largely on volunteer doctors, nurses, and other specialists and workers for their staffing requirements, and on donations for their financial well-being, as well as equipment and supplies. Those who are interested in positions in this system are encouraged to inquire via Sai Baba Websites, or to bring their credentials and apply directly through the ashram at Prasanthi Nilayam.

GENERAL RELIEF SERVICES

One of the unique features of the approach of the Sai Baba organization to solving widespread long-standing problems is the integration of its activities. A cursory overview might imply divisions within the organization that in fact do not exist. Organizers recognize that health issues are not separate from other problems, such as access to transportation, rural poverty, clean water supplies, education, and so on. At first, it might seem that they have taken on every aspect of Indian society, and in a sense, indeed they have. Somehow they appear to maintain a level of coordination that rarely results in collapse because of uneven concentration of attention or of isolation of misidentified problems, as so often happens even in the sophisticated relief efforts of the educated West.

Teams of workers provide guidance and education in rehabilitation centers for troubled youth and orphans, and similar service projects seek to address other of the root causes of social imbalance. When there are natural disasters such as floods and earthquakes, workers are sent to contribute to relief and rebuilding efforts. Educational teams of Sai Baba devotees often visit remote villages to conduct educational campaigns and to support village planning efforts. Some of their activities address unique goals. For one example, anyone acquainted with the ruinous costs of traditional celebrations and dowries that are expected with marriage ceremonies, regardless of economic status, recognizes that these events contribute significantly to the poverty of rural poor and even middle-class urban families: The Sai Baba organization conducts mass marriages, so that couples can start their families within a sanctified and socially acceptable context and without incurring insurmountable debt. In many villages throughout India, Sai Baba devotees are deeply involved in the most basic activities of relief of poverty, such as distribution of donated clothing and food.[35]

DRINKING WATER SUPPLIES

The state of Andhra Pradesh, where Prasanthi Nilayam is located, is subject to the usual seasonal cycles of extreme dryness and heavy monsoon rains. This climate pattern, by no means unique to India, results in a number of phenomena. Villagers will rebuild, year after year, century after century, near the highest part of the water table, which is the low level of the river course in dry season, and they are predictably flooded out every rainy season. Floods are common, and there are often few facilities (such as tanks and reservoirs) for holding precious rain water from the monsoon season to provide a supply for the dry season. Irrigation, where it is applied in remote rural areas, is often of the most primitive kind, such as bucket brigades and drawing from wells. Hygiene is very poorly understood, and populations often drink from the very water in which they wash and bath, in which they water their livestock, and which serves to hold their excretions.

Wells are often cultivation sites for Hansen's disease, tuberculosis, and other microbial infections. Nearly all of rural India, and a high percentage of urban India, suffers from chronic multiple infestations of their gastrointestinal tracts, as a result of unstable and contaminated water resources. Contaminated water sources are the most significant factor contributing to high incidences of eye disease and Hansen's disease throughout south Asia. Few villagers are informed about boiling water to kill bacteria, and there is invariably insufficient fuel for the essential activity of cooking, let alone for sanitization or disinfection.

The Sri Sathya Sai Baba Drinking Water Supply Project resulted from the basic realization that without a safe water supply, all their other efforts in health care and alleviation of rural poverty would be largely ineffective. The scope of the project is truly impressive. The project was begun in 1994, and from its very beginning it was directed by the Sri Sathya Sai Central Trust. The physical plant work was carried out by Larsen & Toubro, Limited, in coordination with the government of the state of Andhra Pradesh. Remarkably, the entire cost of the project thus far, the equivalent of U.S. $63 million, has been donated. Public works projects of this scale, even in an industrialized nation such as the United States, would drag on forever, bogged down in interminable wrangling over water rights, end up serving far fewer than intended, and cost far more than projected.

However, under the Sai Baba Central Trust, an overall attitude of cooperation with private enterprise and governmental authority was established from the outset, with the result that the funds expended were fruitfully utilized almost beyond comprehension. Water service was extended to about 750 villages, with a cumulative population of 900,000 humans and their livestock, and plans are in the works to serve 1,250,000 people. Nearly 270 elevated reservoirs with a capacity of 40,000 to 3000,000 liters each were built, connected to 750 km of main lines by 1,550 km of branch lines, into which were networked 125 ground reservoirs of 20,000 to 60,000 liters each. There are four summer storage reservoirs (called tanks or stations in India) of about 60 acres surface area each, and three more summer storage reservoirs of about 32 acres surface area each.[24]

These reservoirs are supplied by 13 infiltration wells, and 250 bored wells. The bored wells alone supply 274 villages, and almost 100 more villages are covered by 14 protected water supplies with infiltration wells and filter stations. Almost 100 more villages are supplied by the summer tanks, and 115 more villages are supplied with water treatment plants that use water from the Pennar Ahobilam Balancing Reservoir as the primary source. An infiltration well in the bottom of the Chitravathi Balancing Reservoir at Parnapalli supplies an additional 165 villages. These are mere numbers, however. The scope of the project is not within human imagination unless one refers to a map of Andhra Pradesh or visits southern India during the dry season.[36]

As with the healthcare, educational, and poverty-relief service projects, it is evident that the wide base of support the Central Trust enjoys with the Drinking Water Supply Project is directly proportional to the ethical and moral esteem earned by those organizers who actively apply the teachings and ideals of Sai Baba.

9

Embodiment
of Love

*This is a great chance. Be confident that you will all be
liberated. Know that you are saved. Many hesitate to
believe that things will improve, that life will be happy
for all and full of joy, and that the golden age will recur.
Let me assure you that this* dharmaswarupa, *that this
divine body, has not come in vain. It will succeed in
averting the crisis that has come upon humanity.*

—Satya Sai Baba

SRI SATYA
SAI BABA

Sri Satya Sai Baba is shown here as a young man. His transformation from Satya-Narayana to Sri Satya Sai Baba, when he was only 13 years old, occurred when Satya endured a period of physical and mental suffering, possibly resulting from a snake or scorpion bite.

Sai Baba walks through his ashram, allowing himself to be seen by his devotees. This practice is called *darshan*, literally "seeing," and is said to convey blessings by mere presence and not due to any personal interaction.

Sai Baba blesses his disciples as he arrives on a modified vehicle at an event to celebrate his 78th birthday, November 23, 2003. Thousands of believers from all over the world traveled to Puttaparthi to witness the celebrations.

Students relax at the Satya Sai Institute of Higher Learning. Sai Baba founded this university in 1981, to uphold high standards of academic excellence and to develop high moral and ethical standards in its students. Tuition at the university is free, and room and board require a small fee. There are many Sai Baba Institutes around the world that are modeled after the original Institute of Higher Learning.

Sai Baba greets followers after the opening of the Sri Satya Sai Baba International Center in New Delhi, which is intended to promote the appreciation of "world heritage," March 12, 1999. Sai Baba had not visited the city of New Delhi for 17 years before the inauguration of the Center, but he promised to return to the city every year thereafter.

Indian Prime Minister Ata Behari Vajpayee walks with Sai Baba after their meeting in the southern city of Bangalore, April 14, 2004. Vajpayee, who was campaigning for re-election, sought Sai Baba's blessings for his efforts.

Portrait of the guru. Sai Baba defined *guru* as "one who dispels darkness of ignorance" or "one who reveals *Guri* (target) to the disciple." Many of Sai Baba's devotees refer to him as their guru, or spiritual leader.

Today, Sai Baba is perhaps the most renowned holy man, with millions of followers throughout the world. Among his followers are celebrities such as Duchess of York Sara Ferguson, Isaac Tigrett (the founder of the popular Hard Rock Cafe chain), American movie stars Goldie Hawn and Stephen Segal; some have even mentioned Great Britain's Prince Charles of England, former U.S. president Bill Clinton, and Clinton's wife, Senator Hillary Rodham Clinton, as they have all sought Sai Baba's guidance and benedictions.[37] In India, he is perhaps the most popular living person after the prime minister, who is a long-time devotee of Satya Sai Baba. Numerous important Indian spiritual gurus, statesmen, and scientists are among his followers. Because of his immense social, cultural, and political clout, many Indian politicians have bowed before him in hopes of public endorsement. Sai Baba is the most widely followed spiritual guru in India and perhaps in the world. According to some reports, as many as 60 million people outside India are his devotees.[38] He draws followers from people of various religions, ethnicity, and social class. Today, his followers operate Sai Baba Centers all over the world, from Malaysia to the United States.

Sai Baba's residence, Prasanthi Nilayam, is the world's largest ashram for a living guru. It is also the most popular and most frequently visited pilgrimage site in the world, after Mecca and the Vatican. Every day thousands of people come to Puttaparthi in the hope of an opportunity to glimpse the God-incarnate guru during darshans, the set times of the day when Sai Baba shows his face to the eager crowd and blesses them with his presence. Because of the large number of visitors, Sai Baba holds darshans twice a day, once in the morning and once in the afternoon, and people line up hours beforehand to guarantee themselves a good spot. The front seats are popular because from them viewers can better see Sai Baba, and he may say a few words to those who sit there. He may reach out to receive the letters that devotees offer to request guidance on a particular matter, or he may grant requests for a face-to-face visit and interview. Private interviews are very popular because it is during these interviews that Sai Baba materializes objects such as holy ash (vibhuti), rings, watches, necklaces, and miscellaneous trinkets as gifts for his followers. His devotees believe that as long as they keep these gifts with them, they will be blessed by Sai Baba's grace.

Thanks to Sai Baba's popularity and grace, Puttaparthi, once a remote village, has turned into a prosperous town with modern amenities to serve its rapidly growing multinational population. The town boasts a busy airport, a modern railway station, two hospitals, a university, a school, a planetarium, a music school, banks, cafeterias, bookstores, aesthetic gardens, playgrounds, and museums. It is believed that about 10,000 people visit the town on a daily basis, and because the majority of visitors are affluent, they contribute greatly to the town's economy. To serve the visitors, luxury houses, apartment buildings, condominiums, and hotels are springing up, and a brand-new airport is available to serve the wealthier devotees.

Puttaparthi is perhaps the only town in modern times that is the seat of a world-class super-specialty hospital (Sri Sathya Sai Institute of Higher Medical Sciences) equipped with modern state-of-the-art facilities in surgery and medicine to treat patients free of charge. Whoever comes for help is treated free. According to the Sathya Sai Organization, between November 22, 1991, and September 30, 2004, the hospital performed 14,309 heart surgeries, 14,637 catheterization procedures, 24,443 urology surgeries, 24,333 ophthalmology surgeries, and 3,865 CT scans.[39] In relation to the nature and mission of the hospital, Sai Baba states: "When any educational or medical institution is established, the sole aim is to make a business of it. There are few who are ready to set up institutions to provide free facilities for the poor. Therefore, from the start we decided to set up a hospital near Prashanthi Nilayam. Even as higher education is free here, 'higher medicine' also will be free. People spend some lakhs[40] to get heart surgery done in the United States. What is the plight of the poor?

Who looks after them? If they go to the cities, they will not get even basic medicine. Recognizing this fact, we have launched this big hospital project. Whether it is heart bypass operation, a kidney transplant, a lung operation, brain surgery or eye surgery, everything will be done free. This has been decided upon from the very start of the project."[41]

The town also contains a university that comprises three campuses to provide its students with free education in the arts, sciences, business, management, and computer science. Other educational facilities include a music college, a couple of Higher Secondary Schools and several primary and middle schools. Students, Sai Baba believes, are the most valuable human resources: "Students are the foundation of the nation, the only wealth that I cherish. Students are my all; My entire property consists of students; I have offered Myself to them."[42] Sai Baba has made sure that the university curriculum would harmoniously integrate spiritual education with ethical, physical, and metaphysical sciences. The town also houses a planetarium and two museums, one a museum of spiritual traditions (Sri Sathya Sai Sanathana Samskruti) that depicts symbols, saints, and seers of various faiths and religions, and the other one a museum dedicated to the life and times of Sai Baba as a living avatar (Chaitanya Jyoti Museum).

Here one can see that it is not Sai Baba's materialization of objects or other attributed miracles that attract people to him as much as it is his message of love, which is reflected in his humanitarian works. Because in a country like India, where miracles are taken for granted as within the abilities of holy man, and holy men are accepted as a part of everyday life, what stirs the population are not petty miracles here and there, but humane and charitable actions. It is these acts that attract people to Satya Sai Baba and to his message. Sai Baba always refers to his miracles as his "visiting cards," however. Through his miracles, people become curious about him and then are provided with the opportunity to benefit form his divine wisdom. He states:

I am determined to correct you only after informing you of my credentials. That is why I am now and then announcing my Nature by means of miracles, that is, acts which are beyond human capacity and human understanding. Not that I am anxious to show off my Powers. The object is to draw you closer to me, to cement your hearts to me.[43]

During his long career as an avatar, Sai Baba has had a fair number of skeptics who have questioned the validity of his miracles and his claim to divinity. Among the most popular critics is Basava Premanand, the editor and publisher of *The Indian Skeptic*, who totally dismisses Sai Baba as an avatar and calls him a fraud. On his Website, he posts a video of Sai Baba's materialization of gifts, and discards these actions as a magician's acts rather than a divine intervention. Another skeptic, Dale Beyerstein, author of *Sai Baba's Miracle: An Overview*, also questions Sai Baba's legitimacy as an avatar and brands him a magician. He makes a note that if these miracles are truly creations of Sai Baba, he must be in violation of international copyrights laws by materializing brand-name Swiss watches with company logos and serial numbers.[44] A Website on Sai Baba's miracles not only refers to them as magician's acts, but also gives the reader believable instructions and the necessary techniques to produce vibhuti (the sacred ash that Sai Baba often produces), and to swallow a lingam (an egg-like sacred object that Sai Baba abruptly ejected from his mouth into his hand during his early years of avatarhood), and to eject it back at will.[45] There are other accusations of sexual and financial abuses, which all have been rejected by Sai Baba and officials in the Indian government's judicial system.

Perhaps what keeps Sai Baba's mission alive in the face of various controversies and accusations surrounding his life is the enthusiasm of his devotees. With their immense help, Sai Baba has been able to develop his movement into a vast, prosperous, and spirited force. Having powerful devotees among Indian government officials has helped him to develop a close working relationship with the national government of India and to some extent has provided him with immunity from controversies. Funded mainly by his wealthy devotees and supported by the Indian government, today Sai Baba's establishment consists of a gigantic conglomeration of schools, ashrams, colleges, hospitals, and other charitable organizations. The Central Sri Sathya Sai Trust is Sai Baba's legal organization, and it is in charge of receiving donations and managing properties and charitable affairs. Donations can be made at any time and any amount at any branch of the Canara Bank; these will be directly deposited into the Sri Sathya Sai Trust's account. It is interesting to note that Sai Baba himself does not accept any donations and does not own any personal property. He often claims that as an omnipotent creator he is above these human concerns.

Hugh Urban, a scholar who has recently studied Sai Baba, characterizes him as a "distinctly 'modern' kind of guru, radiating an aura of affluence, cosmopolitanism and progress which seems particularly appealing to India's growing and socially ambitious middle classes."[46] He has also been described as "a jet-lag holy man" who constantly travels in automobiles and airplanes to meet his followers in various parts of India. His religious style varies significantly from other known gurus. He tends to resonate with the religious yearnings of the cosmopolitan wealthy. Sai Baba's followers are mainly drawn from a particular segment of contemporary Indian society, characterized as the upwardly mobile, well-educated and Western-influenced middle class. This class is mainly "the affluent, the comfortable, the smart and the up-to-date," and from populous urban centers such as Bombay, Bangalore, and New Delhi.[47]

He has also been described as man of seeming contradictions. Although Westernized in his approach to Western education, technology, and science, he nevertheless repeatedly warns his followers about the decadence of Western materialism and consumerism in the age of global capitalism. He is an outspoken opponent of Westernization and warns his followers against idealizing the West as their model for development. He criticizes the West for its seeming immorality and promiscuity. To him, Western society is decadent and wasteful, and its influence upon India is evil. He refers to the demoralizing and material-istic influence of the modern West as the greatest single cause of the contemporary world's problems and the main threat to traditional societies like that of India, and that this imminent threat must be battled by intellectuals and religious and political leaders in less developed countries. Whereas India is seen by him as the land of religion, mysticism, and inner truth, the West is viewed as the land of atheism, immorality, and spiritual decline. He states that the West has been able to conquer the East, but the price they had to pay was a profound loss of ethical and spiritual ideals. Criticizing India's desire for Western fashion and habits, he warns his followers not to blindly mimic the West and thereby make India into another pseudo-America, obsessed with worldly pleasures. Sai Baba also blames British coloniza-tion of India for corrupting the Indian cultural tradition. Western powers, by captivating the Indian market, became materially prosperous, and material prosperity became the key to their happiness, he argues. Measuring happiness by material posses-sions, as many Westerners do today, is in sharp contrast with Vedic teachings that relate happiness to one's spiritual well-being and tranquility of mind.[48]

Sai Baba argues that although the age of colonialism is over, Indians, like many people of poor nations, are still under the yoke of Western cultural imperialism. The educated class, including many Indian political leaders, is infatuated with Western values, dress, language, opinion, and the entire way of life. They yearn for Western material goods and wealth at the expense of traditional Indian values and religious ideals. He complains about India's cultural dependency upon the West: "The dependence still continues, although we style ourselves as independent. The Sanathana Dharma (eternal path of righteous-ness), which is a diamond necklace on the breast of the mother is discarded and a plastic necklace sought to be substituted."[49]

Sai Baba's followers admire his courage to stand up against Western materialism and secularism, as well as his attempts to bring about much-needed spiritual liberation in a spiritually deprived age. Indian nationalists also admire Sai Baba for his tireless efforts to prevent India from culturally succumbing to the West by standing behind preservation of a Hindu national identity. They believe the time is ripe for an avatar like Sai Baba to rid their country of the evils of Westernization: "The present situation is so alarming that corruption

GOODNESS
Selected from Sai Baba's Discourses

Goodness is not false or impossible but is the one factor which gives the real value of life. Life without goodness is not real life but only a sense of the destructive dance of the evil forces which shall draw individuals into grief. Goodness is the way to true happiness. In the ultimate analysis, there is no separate entity such as goodness. It (goodness) attains the relative plane where duality is transcended—no question of pairs of opposites arises. Goodness is the virtue or conduct which does not violate the oneness of all life.

Boys! Why does God command good acts? There is no question of command from God. He has given all human beings a greater or lesser measure of intelligence and reason and He has also endowed man with conscience. When man exercises all the three gifts of God properly he will find that all his deeds are directed towards goodness. In other words, God doesn't interfere or place any specific command on the nature of action done by anyone. He has left man to do as he likes.

But goodness is the real nature of man, who is only an Image of God. This fact naturally gives a heart to man towards doing good and punishes him with remorse if he swerves from the path of goodness. Man does not live by bread only, he lives by the spirit within him.

What is lawless law? It is a rule of conduct laid down and enforced by mere might and not based on any spiritual considerations.

With Blessings,

Baba
January 26, 1973

in high places, the reign of terrorism, the disruption of family life, promiscuousness in sex, and criminalization in politics are the order of the day. These and other distortions Baba has to correct."[50]

Sai Baba calls for a return to the ancient Hindu social and spiritual principles constituted by sacred texts such as the Vedas and Upanishads. Some argue that a return to traditional Hindu social tenets is to some degree a return to outdated principles, such as a socially unfair caste system and discrimination against females as less valuable members of society. Hindu traditionalism, as interpreted by many of the old sacred scriptures, negates the egalitarianism of the West, which tends to use science and rationalism rather than religious dogma to cure the ills of society. Although one can question the just application of egalitarian principles in the West, one nevertheless cannot dismiss the validity of these ideas in theory. One can, however, argue that Sai Baba's support for Indian nationalism is not the same as those Hindu nationalists who are hostile to non-Hindusm, such as Sikhs, Buddhists, Muslims, and Christians. Only a glance at Sai Baba's organization's logo, which calls for unity of religions and humanity, can attest to this difference.

Some argue that while Sai Baba publicly advocates support for the poor and dispossessed, he has not displayed any serious opposition to the Indian caste system, discrimination against women, or the horrors of child labor and child prostitution that are common in India. Sai Baba's views on the status of women, as depicted from his various discourses, is confusing. He states: "A virtuous woman is a treasure, but she has a circumscribed place in the order of things. Women should strive to realize stri-dharma, the inherent virtues of womanhood, which means they should not be seen or talked about and should stay away from the public gaze; they should be silent invisible partners."[51] One can see here that Sai Baba's view on gender roles differs little from the views of religious conservatives in other parts of the world. One can find similar statements about gender roles in the Christian Bible.

In another statement about proper gender roles, Sai Baba expresses this opinion: "A lady must look after the home first and then work outside, if necessary. . . . she can study to get degrees, enter politics or do any other work but she should not neglect the home, which is the very foundation of her life."[52] Here one can see that there is such a sharp contrast between this statement and the statement about women's roles that was mentioned earlier that it becomes a difficult task for a devotee to form a guided opinion on the topic.

Some observers have noticed that Sai Baba's anti-Western rhetoric is toned down when his audience contains many European or American attendants.[53] There are enough contradictions in Sai Baba's statements to make a serious study of his position on some of the social issues a difficult task. In another word, one cannot often come up with a pattern that is consistent throughout. Despite Sai Baba's many critics, one cannot ignore the positive influence that Sai Baba's life and work has had upon India in general and on his devotees in particular. Many Indian poor have benefited through his generous charitable work with schools, hospitals, and water projects. Also, numerous followers who have spoken or written about him have stated that Sai Baba has given meaning and purpose to their lives by prescribing daily prayers, meditation, charitable work, individual duty, and positive relations with family and community. They have called him "the embodiment of love."[54]

10

A Miracle of the Heart

This is love without boundaries, love without conditions,
love without desiring anything in return.
This is even more perfect than how a mother loves,
and a mother's love is very great!
This is the love the One has for creation,
it is for this love that creation was made.
For others, there are small miracles,
a gold ring or bangle. You do not want such trinkets,
so I invite you to this greatest miracle, pure love.

—Satya Sai Baba

That evening Sarah showed up for a meeting that she had scheduled with a couple of young pilgrims.[55] They were there to converse about Sai Baba and his healing powers. From the start, Sarah realized that she was in a different spiritual place than they were. They made it clear to her that only true believers in Baba would feel the impact of his positive energy. They explained that internal peace and tranquility is only transferred through Baba when a pilgrim is mentally as well as spiritually ready to receive Baba's blessing. So, she was told that if she didn't feel a change from visiting Baba, it was her own problem, not Baba's. They recommended that she leave the ashram, because as long as she remained in disbelief, nothing would change within her.

Later, as she walked along, some pleasant music attracted Sarah's attention. A group of young people were sitting on the ground in a circle, playing music and singing songs. One of the people in the group invited Sarah to join their gathering. After a short introduction, Sarah found out that most of them were medical students from Germany. The young man who played guitar, however, was a computer software student from England. He was the man who invited her to join. One of the young men told Sarah that his father was an official propagator for Sai Baba and his teachings in Germany. When asked about his views of Baba's miracles and grace, he said he was a Catholic and did not believe such things. He mentioned, however, that seeing Baba and reading Baba's books and ideas provides him with a sense of peace and tranquility, and so he and his friends come every year to Puttaparthi for relaxation and to take back beautiful memories with them.

As Sarah departed for her hotel room, she again saw little Pirouz, with his bizarre face, running around with his video camera and acting like he was a real journalist. The boy's young mother, Keshvar, was following him, to make certain that he did not disturb people who didn't want to be bothered by the boy's playfulness or his mischievous behavior. Sarah gazed upon the deformed face of the boy. "What courage he has!" she thought, "Always so cheerful, even when strangers stare at him and other boys refuse to play with him; he always laughs, and is never cruel to others!" After she saw Sarah from a distance, Keshvar walked closer and cheerfully greeted her. She expressed her anxiety about tomorrow, the day that she expected to take her precious, afflicted son to be cured by Sai Baba.

On the next day, the darshan ritual was repeated again, but it was not as fascinating to Sarah as it was the day before. In the crowd, Sarah saw Keshvar dragging her son Pirouz and feverishly pushing people aside in the hope of reaching the front row. She finally managed to secure a space in the front row, and when Baba walked by she handed him an envelope.

Later, Sarah noticed that a group of people wearing clean white attire decorated with shiny green shawls separated themselves from the crowd and formed a line. Sarah located the boy and his mother among them. Because she knew some people in the group, she joined them, and they were all taken to see Baba. The group was guided toward the room where Baba keeps his daily appointments. They were given instructions in how to behave properly during the visit. As they entered the room, Sarah noticed Baba sitting on a large and elegant chair. Around him were statues of Hindu gods. She recognized the elephant-headed statue of Ganesh, the son of Shiva and Parvati, who is widely worshiped in India as the god of wisdom and the remover of obstacles. The other statues familiar to Sarah were of Shiva (the third member of Hindu Trinity, responsible for destruction and regeneration), and Shakti (the divine creative power, cosmic energy, and the personification of male deity in the form of his female consort).

They approached Baba's chair one person at a time, by creeping on their knees. Whoever approached Baba, Sarah noticed, gently touched Baba's feet, and Baba waved his hand to sprinkle his sacred ash on their head, face, and shoulders. As the little boy with the bizarre face approached Baba, Sarah's heart began to pump harder. Deep in her heart, she wished for a miracle. She wished that everything she had heard about Baba's miracles would come true and that he could perform the seemingly impossible. She wished that the lovable little boy would be cured, and that he and his mother would leave the ashram in happiness. As the boy approached Baba's chair, Baba looked at the boy's eyes, said something in his ear, and gave him a ring that seemed to materialize out of thin air.

The private visit with Baba was over, but the boy was still the same! "What happened?" Sarah pondered, "Do miracles really happen?" She felt heartbroken that the boy and his mother did not get their wish. Soon she noticed the mother was holding the boy in her arms and crying loudly. Sarah wanted to shake her and ask her, "So, what happened? The boy looks the same as he did before the meeting!" Some young devotees gathered around the boy and his mother. They ardently kissed the ring in the boy's hand and told his mother that she was lucky to receive a ring from Baba. "Don't ever separate this ring from you; this is your connection with our glorious Baba," they continued. Despite the signs of disappointment in his mother's face, they assured her that Baba's divinity should not be measured by acts alone, "Baba is above these worldly things. Instead of curing the outer appearance of the boy," they argued, "Baba has blessed your boy's inner essence. His inner beauty will shine because of this encounter with Baba, you and your son are lucky to have the blessing of our Lord," they reassured her.

One of the young men reminded the mother of a passage from Sai Baba's divine statements:

I have come to give you the key to the treasure of *ananda* (or bliss), to teach you how to tap that spring, for you have forgotten the way to blessedness. If you waste this time of saving yourselves, it is just your fate. You have come to get from me tinsel and trash, the petty little cures and promotions, worldly joys and comforts. Very few of you desire to get from me the thing that I have come to give you: namely, liberation itself. Even among these few, those who stick to the path of *sadhana*, (or spiritual practice), and succeed are a handful.[56]

Another devotee recited a different passage by Sai Baba: "Many of you come here to me with problems of health and mental worry of one sort or another. They are mere baits by which you have been brought here. But the main purpose is that you may have grace and strengthen your faith in the divine."[57]

After the young devotees were gone, Keshvar was still crying. Sarah stayed, in the hope of soothing her with sympathy and words of encouragement. "Have I traveled so far for nothing? All these thousands of followers . . . how can I come closer to him?" Keshvar fumbled in her bag, looking for something to wipe her tears. Sarah handed her a clean tissue, and gently comforted her. "I have spent the last of our savings to get here," she continued, and then lifted her arms toward the sky and moaned, "I pray, Oh God, for You to reveal to me the reality of my life. I accept the hardness of this life with its blessings as the karma of my past actions in lives veiled to me. You are the All-knowing and All-seeing. Can you reveal to me why my son is so afflicted?" She then turned toward her son, gazed upon his deformed face, and cried out, "With such a face, how will he succeed in life?" Sarah was deeply moved by the woman's frantic prayers and sad lamentations and had a hard time calming her. "Baba, please, please heal my son," the mother begged desperately. The boy was saddened by his mother's sobbing, and in sorrow held her with his two little hands, and implored her, "Mama, please do not worry, I am fine, I am fine!" "But you are not!" she wailed. "You are exactly the same as before!"

As the pale autumn sun disappeared behind the rocky hills of Puttaparthi, the evening twilight upon the reddish hills provided a majestic panorama from Sarah's window, but Sarah was in a melancholy mood. She did not feel like leaving her room or seeing anyone, but she had to eat something before the lights were turned off in the ashram. She reluctantly left for the restaurant, in the hope of at least seeing Keshvar and her son one last time before they left the ashram the next day. At the restaurant, she looked for them but could not find them. "Perhaps they are not in the mood for the restaurant tonight, or perhaps Keshvar is staying home and sobbing, as she has been doing all day," she thought to herself.

The restaurant was crowded, and she could not find an empty table. As she was looking around, she heard a gentle voice inviting her to his table. A tall and good-looking man who seemed to be in his late forties invited her to sit on an empty chair next to him. Sarah thanked the man and took the empty chair. After an introduction and some small talk, Sarah asked the man about his spiritual path and journey. The man, who introduced himself as Bob, smiled and said, "I really don't think that I have a path, and believe it or not, I don't even know why I am here!" "How come?" Sarah asked.

"The truth is that I was tired and I needed a vacation. Last week on a very busy day at work I took a break and went to get coffee. On my way, I looked into the window of a New Age bookstore that I pass by every day. The faces on the covers somehow had a different look that day. I had often passed by the window with barely a glance at its contents. Looking at those strange, cross-legged people, I thought to myself, 'Is there anything of any value in all this? Sitting still and accomplishing nothing, what kind of religion is that?'" He continued, "But that morning, I was disturbed by a different sensation, as if the faces on those covers were not grinning in emptiness, but seemed to sense my deep frustration and longing, as if they knew me and were smiling in gentle kindness.

"Like someone was pushing me, without thinking, I went in, and stopped and looked around. The woman behind the counter looked at me and asked, 'What do you want?' I blushed and stammered, and turned to leave in embarrassment. 'I don't know what I want, I don't know what all this is, really, I wouldn't know where to begin,' and then I noticed that her smile was like one of the figures on the book covers in the window. 'If you don't know what you want, you will have to find out. If you don't know where to begin, you can begin anywhere. You could begin with these,' she said, and handed me three books. The first seemed too simplistic, because it was filled with too many exhortations to 'feel your bliss.' The second looked like more of the same, but it was layered with strange images and exotic paraphernalia, and long passages in undecipherable writings I suspected it would make no sense, even if I could translate them."

"I almost laughed out loud at the third one, For goodness sake, a skinny little guy with a pudgy face and hair like an African-American hipster from the 1970s, wearing a bright orange robe no less! I flipped it open and scanned a few pages. A half-hour later, the saleswoman interrupted my absorption with a cheery, 'What do you think?' 'I think I'll buy this one, actually,' I admitted, 'and please put it in a bag.' 'What would my colleagues think if they saw me reading this? What do I think of me reading this?' I wondered as I went out the door into the bright sunlight."

Sarah listened carefully, and tried to make sense of what Bob was saying. He then continued, "By the next morning, I had made up my mind. I decided to visit Baba's ashram and see with my own eyes the things that I had read about. And now here I am." "So," asked Sarah excitedly, "did you get what you wanted?" Bob shook his head and sighed, "Not really! After three days of meditation and *darshans*, I am feeling more empty and desolate than ever."

There were a few minutes of silence, which Bob broke with the question "You didn't tell me about your journey. What are your feelings about the ashram?" Sarah started talking about her observations and how she, like Bob, felt almost no change in her heart. Their conversation drifted to talk about the little boy and his mother, and how they had been left heartbroken after visiting Baba this morning. Bob suddenly seemed to be extremely interested. "Can I see the boy?" he asked anxiously. "I was hoping to see them here, but I guess they felt too disheartened to come to a crowded place like this," responded Sarah. "Do you know how I can find them?" Bob asks. "Yes, I know where they are staying, and I can take you there," Sarah said. Bob stood up immediately and asked, "Can we please go there now?" Surprised by Bob's unusual excitement, she responded "I guess so."

Sarah and Bob walked toward the old section where the less well-off visitors usually stayed. They found Keshvar and her son in a small room within a large, old house. Keshvar greeted them and invited them in. The room was very small but neat and clean. Keshvar, who looked so attractive and excited the day before, looked very tired this evening. Her eyes were red and sunken, as if she had been crying all day. The little boy, who knew Sarah very well by now, seemed elated to receive her and Bob as company. "Perhaps he is too tired of seeing his mom sobbing all day," Sarah thought. He looked as cheerful and naughty as he ever did. As he smiled radiantly, he revealed a cleft palate and lip, and the huge gap between his teeth extended to his nostrils. His eyes, although bulging and crossed, were very bright. Bob sat the boy upon on his knees, and reached across the boy's face, and examined it for a moment. "OK," he whispered as he thought out loud, "a mandibular extension, a cleft palate repair, a bridge, a repositioning of the zygomatic processes, maybe a repositioned septum, and bone grafts to rebuild the orbital structures; I can handle this easily." Sarah and Keshvar inquisitively listened to him, thinking "What is he trying to do?"

"I can help your son, and I can help you," he said in a confident voice, turning toward Keshvar. "I think I know how to arrange everything," he mumbled, "I need a little help myself, of course, but I assume I have to begin somewhere." These last words he whispered to himself. Noticing the puzzled faces of Keshvar and Sarah, he continued in a gentle voice while holding the little boy close to him as if he was holding his own son. "I am sorry. I should have introduced myself properly earlier. I am Dr. Dennison, and I am a maxillofacial surgeon. I have fixed a lot of faces like your son's, and I believe I can obtain good results with him. The only question is this, should I do what I can here, or take you with me to California where I practice?"

After she heard such kind words from the man, Keshvar could not help herself, but started to cry again, this time in joy. Sarah began to put the pieces of the puzzle together in her mind, and the events happening around her began to make sense. Keshvar finally pulled herself together and thanked the doctor, who could see she now worried about the expense of going to California. The tall doctor smiled gently, and said, "Don't worry about a thing, this is all on me." Then he whispered to himself again, "I have to begin somewhere." By now, Sarah knew very well what Bob was whispering about. As Sarah joyfully watched the gentle doctor playing and chatting with the sweet but afflicted little boy, she smiled in her heart and admitted, "Miracles do happen, but in their own strange way."

To express her appreciation, Keshvar offered the doctor and Sarah some food. Sarah and Bob, after dining together, were too full to eat, but to be polite they shared some food with their hosts. Both Sarah and the doctor noticed that the little boy was adding a lot of pepper to his food. When the doctor asked why he was eating so much pepper, in an excited tone he answered, "Baba told me that pepper will burn out my facial wounds, so I am eating a lot of pepper!" Then he burst into laughter and played with the pepper shaker.

The next morning, Sarah sat on the train and contemplated her recent journey to Baba's ashram. She remembered her conversation with Bob the night before, after they left the little boy and his mother. She had learned that Dr. Robert Dennison was one of the top practitioners and researchers in his field and was well known around the globe for his significant contributions to the development of his field. She thought the boy couldn't get a better doctor! She also remembered how Bob opened his heart and confessed to her his feelings of emptiness and unrelenting depression that he had experienced for so long. He had also told her that after seeing the boy, he knew why he was in Puttaparthi. Sarah remembered saying to Bob how happy she was for bringing him and the boy together, and Bob had told her that perhaps that had been her mission in Baba's ashram as well. As the train began to move, Sarah pondered that perhaps this was the miracle for which she had been waiting herself, the transformation of four yearning hearts coming together, a real miracle of the human heart!

As the train left the station, she noticed a large number of Indians standing around the station while they waited for newcomers, to carry their luggage and become their guides. The shops along the street were filled with pictures and statues of Shiva, Krishna, Rama, Ganesh, Shakti, and many other local gods. There was one god, however, whose pictures were all over the town: the god who owns the town. The god whose fame and reputation, and maybe grace, had brought Sarah, Bob, Keshvar, and the sweet little boy Pirouz to Puttaparthi for a sincere transformation of their hearts: Sri Satya Sai Baba.

APPENDIX

SATYA SAI BABA'S LETTER TO HIS BROTHER
May 25, 1947

(On May 25, 1947, at the age of 20, in response to a letter from his brother who was concerned with what he was doing, Sri Satya Sai Baba wrote the following letter. This letter disclosed his mission.)

My dear One! I received the communication that you wrote and sent; I found in it the surging floods of your devotion and affection, with the undercurrents of doubts and anxiety. Let me tell you that it is impossible to plumb the hearts and discover the natures of jnaanis, yogis, ascetics, saints, sages, and the like. People are endowed with a variety of characteristics and mental attitudes, so each one judges according to his own angle, talks and argues in the light of his own nature. But we have to stick to our own right path, our own wisdom, our own resolution without getting affected by popular appraisal. As the proverb says, it is only the fruit-laden tree that receives the shower of stones from passers-by. The good always provoke the bad into calumny; the bad always provoke the good into derision. That is the nature of this world. One must be surprised if such things do not happen.

The people have to be pitied, rather than condemned. They do not know. They have no patience to judge aright. They are too full of lust, anger, and conceit to see clearly and know fully. So, they write all manner of things. If they only knew, they would not talk or write like that. We, too, should not attach any value to such comments and take them to heart, as you seem to do. Truth will certainly triumph some day. Untruth can never win. Untruth might appear to overpower Truth, but its victory will fade away and Truth will establish itself.

It is not the way of the great to swell when people offer worship and to shrink when people scoff. As a matter of fact, no sacred text lays down rules to regulate the lives of the great, prescribing habits and attitudes that they must adopt. They themselves know the path they must tread; their wisdom regulates and makes their acts holy. Self-reliance, beneficial activity—these two are their special marks. They may also be engaged in the promotion of the welfare of devotees and in allotting them the fruits of their actions. Why should you be affected by tangle and worry, as long as I am adhering to these two? After all, praise and blame of the populace do not touch the Atma, the reality; they can touch only the outer physical frame.

I have a "Task": To foster all mankind and ensure for all of them lives full of bliss (ananda). I have a "Vow": To lead all who stray away from the straight path again into goodness and save them. I am attached to a "work" that I love: To remove the sufferings of the poor and grant them what they lack. I have a "reason to be proud," for I rescue all who worship and adore me, aright. I have my definition of the "devotion" I expect: Those devoted to me have to treat joy and grief, gain and loss, with equal fortitude. This means that I will never give up those who attach themselves to me. When I am thus engaged in my beneficial task, how can my name be tarnished, as you apprehend? I would advise you not to heed such absurd talk. Mahatmas do not acquire greatness through someone calling them so; they do not become small when someone calls them small. Only those low ones who revel in opium and marijuana but claim to be unexcelled yogis, only those who quote scriptural texts to justify their gourmand[ism] and pride, only those who are dry-as-dust scholars exulting in their casuistry and argumentative skill—only those will be moved by praise or blame.

You must have read life stories of saints and divine personages; in those books, you must have read of even worse falsehoods and more heinous imputations cast against them. This is the lot of mahatmas everywhere, at all times. Why then do you take these things so much to heart? Have you not heard of dogs that howl at the stars? How long can they go on? Authenticity will win.

I will not give up my mission, nor my determination. I know I will carry them out. I treat the honor and dishonor, the fame and blame that may be the consequence, with equal equanimity. Internally, I am unconcerned. I act but in the outer world; I talk and move about for the sake of the outer world and for announcing my coming to the people; else, I have no concern even with these.

I do not belong to any place; I am not attached to any name. I have no "mine" or "thine." I answer whatever the name you use. I go wherever I am taken. This is my very first vow. I have not disclosed this to anyone so far. For me, the world is something afar, apart. I act and move only for the sake of mankind. No one can comprehend my glory, whoever he is, whatever his method of inquiry, however long his attempt.

You can yourself see the full glory in the coming years. Devotees must have patience and forbearance. I am not concerned, nor am I anxious, that these facts should be known. I have no need to write these words; I wrote them because I felt you would be pained if I do not reply.

Thus, your Baba

Source: *http://www.sathyasai.org/intro/babaslet.htm.*

SATYA SAI BABA'S MISSION
Discourse by Sai Baba on His 43rd Birthday,
November 23, 1968

For the protection of the virtuous, for the destruction of evildoers and for establishing righteousness on a firm footing, I incarnate from age to age. Whenever *asanthi*, or disharmony, overwhelms the world, the Lord will incarnate in human form to establish the modes of earning *prasanthi*, or peace, and to reeducate the human community in the paths of peace. At the present time, strife and discord have robbed peace and unity from the family, the school, the society, the religions, the cities and the state.

The arrival of the Lord is also anxiously awaited by saints and sages. *Sadhus* (spiritual aspirants) prayed and I have come. My main tasks are fostering of the Vedas (Hindu scriptures) and fostering of the devotees. Your virtue, your self-control, your detachment, your faith, your steadfastness: these are the signs by which people read of my glory. You can lay claim to be a devotee only when you have placed yourself in my hands fully and completely with no trace of ego. You can enjoy the bliss through the experience the Avatar confers. The Avatar behaves in a human way so that mankind can feel kinship, but rises into his superhuman heights so that mankind can aspire to reach the heights, and through that aspiration actually reach him. Realizing the Lord within you as the motivator is the task for which he comes in human form.

Avatars like Rama and Krishna had to kill one or more individuals who could be identified as enemies of the dharmic (righteous) way of life, and thus restore the practice of virtue. But now there is no one fully good, and so who deserves the protection of God? All are tainted by wickedness, and so who will survive if the Avatar decides to uproot? Therefore, I have come to correct the buddhi, the intelligence, by various means. I have to counsel, help, command, condemn and stand by as a friend and well-wisher to all, so that they may give up evil propensities and, recognizing the straight path, tread it and reach the goal. I have to reveal to the people the worth of the Vedas, the *Sastras* and the spiritual texts which lay down the norms. If you will accept me and say "Yes," I too will respond and say, "Yes, yes, yes." If you deny and say "No,"

I also echo "No." Come, examine, experience, have faith. That is the method of utilizing me.

I do not mention Sai Baba in any of my discourses, but I bear the name as Avatar of Sai Baba. I do not appreciate in the least the distinction between the various appearances of God: Sai, Rama, Krishna, etc. I do not proclaim that this is more important or that the other is less important. Continue your worship of your chosen God along lines already familiar to you; then you will find that you are coming nearer to me. For all names are mine, and all forms are mine. There is no need to change your chosen God and adopt a new one when you have seen me and heard me.

Every step in the career of the Avatar is predetermined. Rama came to feed the roots of sathya, or truth, and dharma, or righteousness. Krishna came to foster *shanti*, or peace, and *prema*, or love. Now all these four are in danger of being dried up. That is why the present Avatar has come. The dharma that has fled to the forests has to be led back into the villages and towns. The anti-dharma that is ruining the villages and towns must be driven back into the jungle.

I have come to give you the key of the treasure of *ananda*, or bliss, to teach you how to tap that spring, for you have forgotten the way to blessedness. If you waste this time of saving yourselves, it is just your fate. You have come to get from me tinsel and trash, the petty little cures and promotions, worldly joys and comforts. Very few of you desire to get from me the thing that I have come to give you: namely, liberation itself. Even among these few, those who stick to the path of *sadhana*, or spiritual practice, and succeed are a handful.

Your worldly intelligence cannot fathom the ways of God. He cannot be recognized by mere cleverness of intelligence. You may benefit from God, but you cannot explain Him. Your explanations are merely guesses, attempts to cloak your ignorance in pompous expressions. Bring something into your daily practice as evidence of your having known the secret of the higher life from me. Show that you have greater brotherliness. Speak with more sweetness and self-control. Bear defeat as well as victory with calm resignation. I am always aware of the future and the past as well as the present of every one of you, so I am not so moved by mercy. Since I know the past, the background, the reaction is different.

It is your consequence of evil deliberately done in the previous birth, and so I allow your suffering to continue, often modified by some little compensation. I do not cause either joy or grief. You are the designer of both these chains that bind you. I am *anandaswarupa* (the embodiment of bliss). Come, take *ananda* (bliss) from me, dwell on that *ananda* and be full of *shanti* (peace).

My acts are the foundations on which I am building my work, the task for which I have come. All the miraculous acts which you observe are to be interpreted so. The foundation for a dam requires a variety of materials. Without these it will not last and hold back the waters. An incarnation of the Lord has to be used in various ways by man for his uplift. The Lord has no intention to publicize Himself. I do not need publicity, nor does any other Avatar of the Lord. What are you daring to publicize? Me? What do you know about me? You speak one thing about me today and another tomorrow. Your faith has not become unshakable. You praise me when things go well, and blame me when things go wrong. When you start publicity, you descend to the level of those who compete in collecting plenty by decrying others and extolling themselves. Where money is calculated, garnered or exhibited to demonstrate one's achievements, I will not be present. I come only where sincerity and faith and surrender are valued. Only inferior minds will revel in publicity and self-aggrandizement. These have no relevance in the case of Avatars.

Avatars need no advertisement. The establishment of dharma (righteousness): that is my aim. The teaching of dharma, the spread of dharma: that is my object. These miracles as you call them are just a means toward that end. Some of you remark that Ramakrishna Paramahansa (an Indian saint) said that *siddhis* or yogic powers are obstructions in the path of the *sadhaka* (spiritual aspirant). Yes, siddhis may lead the *sadhaka*, the spiritual aspirant, astray. Without being involved in them he has to keep straight on. His ego will bring him down if he yields to the temptation of demonstrating his yogic powers.

That is the correct advice which every aspirant should heed. But the mistake lies in equating me with a *sadhaka*, like the one whom *Ramakrishna* wanted to help, guide and warn. These *siddhis* or yogic powers are just in the nature of the Avatar—the creation of things with intent to protect and to give joy, is spontaneous and lasting. Creation, preservation and dissolution can be accomplished only by the Almighty, no one else.

Cynics carp without knowledge. If they learn the *Sastras* or scriptures, or if they cultivate direct experience, they can understand me. Your innate laziness prevents you from the spiritual exercises necessary to discover the nature of God. This laziness should go. It has to be driven out of man's nature in whatever shape it appears. That is my mission. My task is not merely to cure and console and remove individual misery, but it is something far more important. The removal of misery and distress is incidental to my mission. My main task is the reestablishment of the Vedas and Sastras (spiritual scriptures), and revealing the knowledge about them to all people. This task will succeed. It will not be limited. It will not be slowed down. When the Lord decides and wills, his divine will cannot be hindered.

You must have heard people say that mine is all magic. But the manifestation of divine power must not be interpreted in terms of magic. Magicians play their tricks for earning their livelihood, worldly fame, and wealth. They are based on falsehood and they thrive on deceit, but this body could never stoop to such a low level. This body has come through the Lord's resolve to come. That resolve is intended to uphold the *sathya*, or truth. Divine resolve is always true resolve. Remember there is nothing that divine power cannot accomplish. It can transmute earth into sky and sky into earth. To doubt this is to prove that you are too weak to grasp great things, the grandeur of the universe.

I have come to instruct all in the essence of the Vedas, to shower on all this precious gift, to protect the *sanathana dharma*, the ancient wisdom, and preserve it. My mission is to spread happiness, and so I am always ready to come among you not once, but twice or thrice, as often as you want me. Many of you probably think that since people from all parts of India, and even foreign countries outside India, come to Puttaparthi, they must be pouring their contributions into the coffers of the Nilayam [Prasanthi Nilayam: name of Sai Baba's ashram]. But let me declare the truth. I do not take anything from anyone except love and devotion. This has been my consistent practice for the last many years. People who come here are giving me just the wealth of faith, devotion and love. That is all.

Many of you come to me with problems of health and mental worry of one sort or another. They are mere baits by which you have been brought here. But the main purpose is that you may have grace and strengthen your faith in the divine. Problems and worries are really to be welcomed as they teach you the lessons of humility and reverence. Running after external things produces all this discontent. That type of desire has no end. Once you have become a slave to the senses, they will not leave hold until you are dead. It is an unquenchable thirst. But I call you to me and even grant worldly boons so that you may turn Godward. No Avatar has done like this before, going among the masses, counseling them, guiding them, consoling them, uplifting them and directing them along the path of *sathya, dharma, shanti* and *prema* (truth, righteousness, peace and love).

My activities and movements will never be altered, whoever may pass whatever opinion on them. I shall not modify my plans for *dharmasthapana* (the establishment of righteousness), my discourses or my movements. I have stuck to this determination for many years and I am engaged in the task for which I have come: that is, to inculcate faith in the path of *prasanthi* (the highest spiritual peace). I shall not stop nor retract a step.

Not even the biggest scientist can understand me by means of his laboratory knowledge. I am always full of bliss. Whatever may happen, nothing can come in the way of my smile. That is why I am able to impart joy to you and make your burden lighter. I never exult when I am extolled, nor shrink when I am reviled. Few have realized my purpose and significance, but I am not worried. When things that are not in me are attributed to me, why should I worry? When things that are in me are mentioned, why should I exult? For me it is always, "Yes, yes, yes." If you give all and surrender to the Lord, he will guard you and guide you.

The Lord has come for just this task. He is declaring that He will do so, and that it is the very task that has brought Him here. I know the agitations of your heart and its aspirations, but you do not know my heart. I react to the pain that you undergo and to the joy that you feel, for I am in your heart. I am the dweller in the temple of every heart. Do not lose contact and company, for it is only when the coal is in contact with the live embers that it can also become live ember. Cultivate a nearness with me in the heart and it will be rewarded. Then you too will acquire a fraction of that supreme love. This is a great chance. Be confident that you will all be liberated. Know that you are saved. Many hesitate to believe that things will improve, that life will be happy for all and full of joy, and that the golden age will recur. Let me assure you that this *dharmaswarupa*, that this divine body, has not come in vain. It will succeed in averting the crisis that has come upon humanity.

Source: *http://www.saibabamiracles.com/baba/mission.html.*

TENFOLD PATH TO DIVINITY
By Sai Baba

1. **Love and serve the homeland; do not hate or hurt the homeland of others.**

   Have a sense of pride in your motherland. Just as your mother has given birth to you, so too the land has given birth to you. Whatever country you belong to, you should have a sense of patriotism. You should not indulge in criticizing other countries or people belonging to other nations. Having trust and faith in your own country, you won't try to put down any other country. Never bring grief or sorrow to your country. To have pride in your own motherland is important.

2. **Honor every religion; each is a pathway to the one God.**

   Never have hatred toward any religion. Honor and respect all religions equally. Even as you are a citizen of your motherland but respect all countries, also respect all religions equally.

3. **Love all without distinction; know that mankind is a single community.**

   Develop a sense of the brotherhood of man. Look upon each person as your own brother or sister. There is only one caste, the caste of humanity. All of us belong to the human race, so everyone is equal. Therefore, love each one equally.

4. **Keep your home and its environs clean; it will ensure health and happiness for you and for society.**

   Keep your own house and its surroundings pure and clean. This hygiene will keep you healthy and benefit your worldly life.

5. **Do not throw coins when beggars stretch their hands for alms; help them to become self-reliant. Provide food and shelter, love and care, for the sick and aged.**

   Be discriminating when dispensing charity. In the name of charity or philanthropy, we tend to do injustice to one's country. Charity does not mean that the land should be full of beggars. We can provide some support and means for the beggars, but provide food, clothing and other conveniences in such a way that you are not encouraging laziness and begging.

6. **Do not tempt others by offering bribes or demean yourself by accepting bribes.**

   Never give or take a bribe. Giving bribes, or accepting bribes, is contrary to the very name of the Sri Sathya Sai Organizations. Bear this in mind continuously.

7. **Do not develop jealousy, hatred or envy on any count.**

   We must seek ways to solve difficulties such as hatred, envy and jealousy. To curb this sense of envy and jealousy, we must develop a broader outlook. Do not differentiate on the basis of race, caste, creed, or country. Follow your cultural and religious customs in your own home, but do not attempt to impose them on society. Rather than this, love each person as your own brother or sister, not seeing him or her as belonging to another creed, religion, or country.

8. **Do not depend on others to serve your personal needs; become your own servant before proceeding to serve others.**

   Develop self-reliance. Members of the Sri Sathya Sai Organizations should do things by themselves; they should not depend on others. You may be very wealthy and have servants and assistants to help in a few tasks, but your own work you must do yourself. If you wish to be of service to society, serve yourself first. One who will not serve society has no right to belong to a Sri Sathya Sai Organization.

9. **Observe the laws of the state and be an exemplary citizen.**

   You should never go against the law of the land. We must follow the letter of the law. The members of the Sri Sathya Sai

Organizations should follow the law in spirit also and be models for the government.

10. **Adore God, abhor sin.**

You must love God and avoid sin. Love God incessantly.

Source: *http://www.eaisai.com/baba/.*

1835 Birth of Shirdi Sai Baba at Parthri, Marathwada.

1918 **October 15:** Death of Shirdi Sai Baba at Shirdi in Maharashtra.

1926 **November 11:** Sri Satya Sai Baba is born in the village of Puttaparthi in the Anantapur District of Andhra Pradesh in Southern India, with the given name Satya-Narayana.

1934–1937 Baba attends elementary school in Puttaparthi and Bukkapatnam; Baba joins Uravakonda High School.

1940 **March 8:** Baba is believed to be bitten by a scorpion; his mental metamorphosis begins.

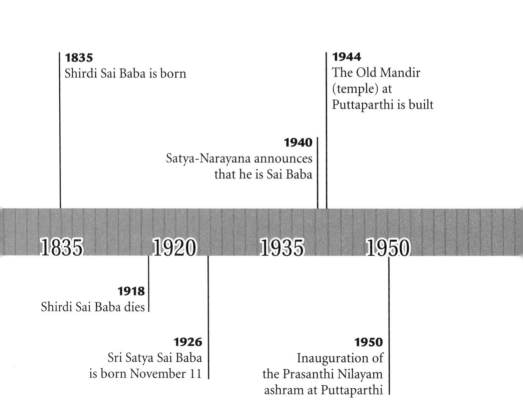

1835
Shirdi Sai Baba is born

1944
The Old Mandir (temple) at Puttaparthi is built

1940
Satya-Narayana announces that he is Sai Baba

1835 1920 1935 1950

1918
Shirdi Sai Baba dies

1926
Sri Satya Sai Baba is born November 11

1950
Inauguration of the Prasanthi Nilayam ashram at Puttaparthi

1940   **May 23:** Baba announces: "I am Sai Baba."

1940   **October 20:** Baba denounces his birth family and claims to be an incarnation of God.

1944   The Old Mandir (temple) at Puttaparthi is built.

1947   **May 25:** In a historic letter to his brother, Baba declares his mission and determination.

1950   **November 25:** Inauguration of Prasanthi Nilayam (Abode of Peace) ashram at Puttaparthi.

1956   **October 4:** Inauguration of Sri Sathya Sai Hospital at Prasanthi Nilayam.

1967
Prasanthi Nilayam is
declared a township

2000
A museum celebrating the
life and works of Baba,
Chaitanya Jyoti, opens

1968
First World Conference
of the Sri Satya Sai Seva
Organization in Bombay

1965   1995   2000

1991
Inauguration of
Sri Satya Sai Institute of
Higher Medical Sciences

1997
First Sri Satya Sai
World Youth Conference

1995
Inauguration
of Sri Satya Sai
Water Supply Project

CHRONOLOGY

1962 **October 16:** Inauguration of All India Prasanthi Vidwan Maha Sabha.

1963 **August 6:** Baba takes upon himself the paralysis of a devotee; he also announces that he is Shiva-Shakthi Swaroopa.

1964 **April 13:** Establishment of a new ashram at Brindavan.

1967 **August 4:** Prasanthi Nilayam is declared a township.

1968 **May 16:** First World Conference of Sri Satya Sai Seva Organization at Bombay; Baba explains in detail about His Incarnation and Mission.

1968 **July:** Baba Visits Uganda, Tanzania, and Kenya.

1968 **July 22:** Inauguration of Sri Satya Sai Arts and Science College for Women at Anantapur.

1972 **May:** Baba gives his first summer course in Indian culture and spirituality.

1975 **November 23:** Inauguration of Sarva Dharma Aikya Stupa; Second World Conference of Sri Satya Seva Organizations at Baba's 50th Birthday.

1976 **August 28:** Inauguration of Sri Satya Hospital at Whitefield.

1979 **July 1:** Inauguration of Sri Satya Sai College, Prasanthi Nilayam.

1980 **November 23:** Baba's 55th birthday: the Third World Conference of Sri Satya Sai Seva Organizations.

1981 **November 22:** Inauguration of Sri Satya Sai Institute of Higher Learning (called the University at Prasanthi Nilayam).

1984 **April 26:** Inauguration of Trayee Brindavan—Bhagawan's new mandir (temple) at Brindavan, Bangalore.

1985 **November 23:** Baba's 60th Birthday: Fourth World Conference of Sri Satya Sai Seva Organizations.

1990   **November 23:** Baba's 65th Birthday: Fifth World Conference of Sri Satya Sai Seva Organizations.

1991   **November 17:** Inauguration of Sri Satya Sai Airport, Prasanthi Nilayam.

1991   **November 22:** Inauguration of Sri Satya Sai Institute of Higher Medical Sciences (Super Specialty Hospital) at Prasanthi Nilayam.

1995   **July 12:** Inauguration of Sri Satya Sai Water Supply Project (Stage 1).

1995   **November 18:** Inauguration of Sri Satya Sai Water Supply Project (Stage 2).

1995   **November 23:** Inauguration of Sri Satya Sai Water Supply Project (Stage 3) by Dr. Shankar Dayal Sharma, President of India at Baba's 70th Birthday; Sixth World Conference of Sri Satya Sai Seva Organization.

1997   **July 16:** First Sri Satya Sai World Youth Conference.

1999   **November 18:** Second Sri Satya Sai World Youth Conference.

2000   **November 1:** Commencement of Rural Services by the students and staff of the university.

2000   **November 18:** Inauguration of Chaitanya Jyoti, a museum on the life and works of Satya Sai Baba.

2000   **November 20:** Inauguration of Sai Mirpuri College of Music at Prasanthi Nilayam.

2000   **November:** Baba's 75th Birthday Celebrations; Seventh World Conference of Sri Satya Sai Seva Organizations.

2001   **January 19:** Inauguration of Super Specialty Hospital at Bangalore.

2004   **November 23:** Baba's 79th Birthday Celebration at Prasanthi Nilayam.

NOTES

CHAPTER 1:
Appointment with a Living God

1. The inspiration for writing this chapter partly came from an article by Mozhgan Ilanloo, who published her observations of a recent trip to Sai Baba's ashram in an Iranian daily paper. The names in the story, however, have been changed. For Ilanloo's article see: Mozhgan Ilanloo, "Gozarehe Safare Hend: Didar ba Sai Baba (Indian Trip Report: Meeting with Sai Baba)," in *Rooznameh Sharq* (Sharq Newspaper), No. 177, May 1, 2004, Page 13.

2. Michael Wood, *Legacy: A Search for the Origins of Civilizations*. Network Books, 1992.

CHAPTER 2:
Miracle Child

3. For a detailed study of life and ideas of Sai Baba, see N. Kasturi, *The Life of Bhagavan Sri Sathya Sai Baba*. 4 vols. Whitefield, India: Sri Sathya Sai Educational and Publication Foundation, 1977, or Kasturi, *The Life of Bhagavan Sri Sathya Sai Baba*, Series on the Life of Sathya Sai Baba. Sathya Sai Book Center of America, 1989. Some accounts of his life can also be read in Marcelo Berenstein, *Sai Baba for Beginners*. Writers and Readers Publishing, 1998.

CHAPTER 3:
Challenges of Childhood

4. N. Kasturi, *Sathyam Shivam Sundaram: The Life of Bhagavan Sri Sathya Sai Baba*.

5. Ibid.

6. For a torturous treatment of Satya during this period, see also Howard Murphet, *Sai Baba: Man of Miracles*, Samuel Weiser, 1987, or Tal Brooke, *Riders of the Cosmic Circuit: Rajneesh, Sai Baba, Muktananda Gods of the New Age*, A Lion Paperback, 1986.

7. N. Kasturi, *Sathyam Shivam Sundaram: The Life of Bhagavan Sri Sathya Sai Baba*.

CHAPTER 4:
The Road to Godhood

8. N. Kasturi, *Sathyam Shivam Sundaram: The Life of Bhagavan Sri Sathya Sai Baba*.

9. Ibid.

10. See Kasturi. Also, some events of his life are recorded by Tal Brooke.

11. N. Kasturi, *Sathyam Shivam Sundaram: The Life of Bhagavan Sri Sathya Sai Baba*.

12. There are many insightful communications between Satya and his older brother Seshama. Perhaps the best one is Satya's letter to his brother on May 25, 1947, in which he articulates his divine mission and worldview. See Appendix for the complete content of this very interesting letter.

13. According to Arnold Schulman, who has interviewed Satya Sai Baba's childhood friends, his childhood life was not so different from his friends'. Many of these stories, he believes, are fabricated by his pious devotees. He also mentions that Sai Baba had a policy of not encouraging his former classmates to come to his ashram. See Arnold Schulman, *Baba*, The Viking Press, 1971.

14. N. Kasturi, *Sathyam Shivam Sundaram: The Life of Bhagavan Sri Sathya Sai Baba*.

15. Ibid.

CHAPTER 5:
Establishment of Divinity

16. Murphet.

17. Kasturi.

18. Murphet.

19. Ibid.

20. Kasturi.

CHAPTER 6:
Avatar of the Age

21. This could be interpreted as the creation of Earth by Parabrahman (The Supreme Creator) with a major sound OM (Aum) or the Big Bang, the most widely accepted cosmological theory in the West.

22. See Appendix for Sai Baba's explanation of the impact of this event in his new transformation. See also *http://www .sathyasai.org/discour/1963/d63076.*

23. It should be noted that Sai Baba of Shirdi never claimed to be an avatar or an incarnation of Shiva, even if some of his devotees claimed that he was, and insisted he was only a "fakir or an obedient servant of God."

24. See *http://www.cosmicharmony.com/Av/ SatyaS2/SatyaS2.htm.*

25. Ibid.

CHAPTER 7:
Teachings and Followers

26. The full texts of the Four Principles, the Nine-point Code of Conduct, the Tenfold Path to Divinity, and the Threefold Objectives can be found at *http://www.sathyasai.org/.*

27. A detailed account of Sai Baba's teachings and discourses are available in a multi-volume set of books titled *Sathya Sai Speaks.* They are also available at *http://www.sathyasai.org/.* These books have been translated into many languages.

28. Another interpretation of the word *Ram* is that *Ra* is the Fire Principle, which burns all to ash, while *ma* stands for "maya" or "illusion," so together, they mean the destruction of illusion. Sai Baba has also said that *Rama* means "He who pleases, fills with bliss, causes delight," and that *Rama* means the joy that comes from love.

29. For a detailed discourse about this and other mantras see *Sathya Sai Speaks* (Discourses of June 5, 1995; June 20, 1977; and March 17, 1983).

30. Sai Baba's teachings about how to prepare for meditation are highly detailed and are derived from ages-old yogic traditions of India. For further study of meditation, see *Sathya Sai Speaks,* volumes 7, 5, and 10.

31. These benefits of reciting any divine name have been enumerated from the *Discourses of Sathya Sai Baba,* and are also found in J. Colamassi, P.K. Prabhakar, and P.K. Swaminathan, *Bhagavan Baba on Namasmarana.*

32. Historically, the mystics of Islam probably borrowed this meditative tool from India when they first encountered the Hindus (bead garlands were also used for meditation in ancient central Asia), and in turn the Catholics borrowed it from them, as the rosary, when Muslims conquered the Iberian Peninsula.

33. The names are listed in N. Kasturi, *Garland of 108 Precious Names.*

CHAPTER 8:
Love All, Serve All: Humanitarian Works

34. *Sathya Sai Speaks.* XI, chapter 31, p. 177, and chapter 36, p. 202; IX, chapter 11, p. 59.

35. For information about contributions by the Sai Baba's charity organizations to the victims of the recent (Dec. 26th 2004) tsunami that hit southeast Asia and parts of India see "Tsunami Relief Work undertaken by Bhagawan Sri Sathya Sai Baba" at *http://www.srisathyasai.org.in/.*

36. Ibid.

CHAPTER 9:
Embodiment of Love

37. Rayal Nair "New Allegations of Abuse Against Sai Baba," *Asian Voice,* June 26, 2004, *http://home.hetnet.nl/~ex_baba/ engels/photo's/asianvoice.jpg.*

38. Stephanie Stallings, "Avatar of Stability," *Harvard International Review,* vol. 22, no. 2 (Summer 2000).

39. See Statistics on Patients and Operations performed at *http://www.sathyasai.org/ saihealth/pnhosp.htm.*

40. In Hindi, *lakh* is a unit of numerical measurement equal to 100,000. For example 550,000 = 5 lakhs + 50,000.

41. See Sai Baba's words on the Sri Sathya Sai Institute of Higher Medical Sciences at *http://www.sathyasai.org/saihealth/pnhosp. htm#Swamis%20words.*

42. Sathya Sai Baba, in *Sathya Sai Speaks,* XI, chap. 36, p. 202; XI, chap. 11, p. 59; XI, chap. 36, p. 206 (old edition).

NOTES

43. See Our Part in the Mission *http://www .cosmicharmony.com/Av/SatyaS2/SatyaS2.htm.*

44. See "Sai Baba: God-man or con man?" by Tanya Datta at *http://news.bbc.co.uk/1/ hi/programmes/this_world/3813469.stm.*

45. See "Materialization" at *http://home.hetnet .nl/~ex_baba/engels/articles/p_holbach/db booke/5mater.htm.*

46. Hugh B. Urban, "Avatar for Our Age: Sathya Sai Baba and the Cultural Contradictions of Late Capitalism," in *Religion,* 33 (2003).

47. See L. Babb, *Redemptive Encounters: Three Modern Styles in the Hindu Tradition,* Berkeley, CA: University of California Press, Berkeley, 1986.

48. For more information about Sai Baba's views on Indian culture vs. Western culture see S.D. Kalkarni, *Shri Sathya Sai Baba: The Font of Vedic Culture.* Bhisma, 1992.

49. For complete study of life and ideas of Sai Baba, see Kasturi, *Sathyam Shivam Sundaram: The Life of Bhagavan Sri Sathya Sai Baba.*

50. S.D. Kalkarni, *Shri Sathya Sai: The Yugavatara.* Bhisma, 1990.

51. Babb, *Redemptive Encounters: Three Modern Styles in the Hindu Tradition,* Berkeley, CA: University of California Press, Berkeley, 1986.

52. *Sanathana Sarathi* (December 1997), pp. 327–328. See also *http://home.no.net/ anir/Sai/enigma/SBWomen.htm.*

53. Hugh B. Urban, "Avatar for Our Age: Sathya Sai Baba and the Cultural Contradictions of Late Capitalism," in *Religion,* 33 (2003).

54. For example, see Peggy Mason and Ron Laing, *Sai Baba: The Embodiment of Love,* Gateway Books, 1996.

CHAPTER 10:
A Miracle of the Heart

55. To better follow the events of this chapter, you need to read Chapter 1 of this book. Chapter 10 is a fictionalized continuation of Sarah's story. The events in this chapter are based on many inspirational accounts of Sai Baba's devotees reported in various books and websites. The characters here are, however, fictional. For various stories by Sai Baba's devotees see: Judy Warner, *Transformation of the Heart: Stories by Devotees of Sathya Sai Baba,* Red Wheel/Weiser, Boston, MA,1995. For similar stories see also: Sathya Sai Baba - Devotee's Stories at: *http://www.cosmicharmony.com/Av/ SatyaSai/SatyaSai.htm*

56. See Kalki Avatar at *http://www .cosmicharmony.com/Av/SatyaS2/ SatyaS2.htm.*

57. Ibid.

ahimsa—Non-violence.

ananda—Joy; bliss; happiness; eternal peace.

arati—To offer a camphor flame before one's guru or deity.

asanti (ashanti)—Discord; turmoil; lack of peace.

ashram—Shelter; haven; a meeting place or residence for spiritual aspirants.

atma (atman)—Self, soul, and universal soul.

avatar—An embodiment; a bodily manifestation of the Divine; descent of God; incarnation.

Baba—A Persian (Urdu) term meaning father; also a title for a guru.

Bhagavan—Lord, God, Divine, and Venerable.

Bhagavad Gita—The Song of God, section of Mahabharata containing spiritual messages of Lord Krishna during his dialogue with Prince Arjuna.

bhajan—Devotional song or hymn.

bhakti—Union with God through devotion, self-surrender.

bhakti yoga—Path of devotion.

Bharat—India.

Brahma—A Creator God, the Absolute.

Brahman—World-soul; the highest caste in Hinduism.

chakra—Wheel; discus; circle; the seven centers of potential energy on the body.

darshan (darsan)—Seeing; viewing; the act of giving an audience to devoteesby a saint or a revered person.

aharma—Duty; nature; a code of ethics righteousness.

fakir (faqir)—A Muslim holy man; ascetic; similar to sannyasin.

gita—Song.

guru—Respected teacher and spiritual guide.

Hari (Hare)—The name of Vishnu, the basic being of the universe.

jnana—Knowledge; wisdom; insight.

jnana yoga—Union with God through wisdom.

GLOSSARY

Kali—Goddess of distraction; another name for Parvati, consort of Shiva.

kali yoga—The present age characterized by decline and deterioration.

Kalki—The Tenth incarnation of Vishnu, born towards the end of kali yoga age.

kama—Fulfilling the legitimate pleasures of life; sexual desire.

karma—Action, deed; the Law of Karma is the law of cause and effect.

Kamasutra—A text about the art of pleasure.

karma yoga—Union with God through selfless acts.

Krishna—Dark; the Eighth incarnation of Vishnu.

Lila (**Leela**)—Miracle; divine sport.

lingam—An oval-shaped symbol of the Absolute.

Mahabharata—A long Sanskrit epic of ancient India that includes the Bhagavad Gita.

mahatama—A great being or soul.

mandir—Temple.

mantra—A word or group of sacred words having power to illumine the mind.

maya—Illusion, ignorance; erroneous perception; the perceptible world.

moksha—Liberation; freedom from all bondage.

Namavali—A lyrical string of names expressing divine attributes or the nature of the Divinity.

Om (**Aum**)—A syllable chanted in meditation, an Upanishadic symbol unfolding the Absolute.

pradesh—Region.

prasanthi—Perfect peace or bliss.

prema—Love; devotion.

pja—Worship.

Ram (**Rama**)—The Seventh incarnation of Vishnu.

Sadhaka—Spiritual aspirants, students or seekers of spiritual knowledge.

samadhi—Tomb; absorption in the Absolute.

samsara—A life of limited existence, of joys and sorrows; the world.

Sanathana Dharma—A way of life followed to discover the Absolute; another name for Hinduism.

sanyasin—A male or female ascetic.

Satya (**Sathya**)—Truth; true.

seva—Service, usually rendered to others.

shakti (**shakthi or sakti**)—Power; power of creation.

sahnti—Peace, tranquility.

Shiva—The god of destruction in the Hindi Trinity.

Sita—White; the consort of Rama.

siddhi—Ascetically acquired power.

Sri (**Sheri**)—Auspicious; title of respect before male name.

Sundara(**m**)—Beauty; splendor; the name of Sai Baba's ashram in Madras.

Suwami—Master; teacher; form of addressing gurus like Sai Baba.

swaroopa—Embodiment, essential nature.

swa-swaroopa—One's own truth or reality.

Tantra—Mystical and magical ritual elements used in techniques for worship among Buddhsts and Hindus.

Veda (**s**)—Knowledge, the earliest Hindu scriptures revealed to the ancient spiritual seers (*rishis*).

Vedanta—The end of the Vedas; final knowledge of Vedas.

Vibhuti—Sacred ash; a manifestation of divine glory.

Vidya—Learning; knowledge.

Yoga—Union with the universal soul.

BIBLIOGRAPHY

Babb, Lawrence, *Redemptive Encounters: Three Modern Styles in the Hindu Tradition (Comparative Studies in Religion and Society Series, No. 1)*, University of California Press, Berkley, 1991.

Berenstein, Marcelo, *Sai Baba for Beginners*, Writers and Readers Publishing, Inc., New York, 1998.

Brooke Tal, *Riders of the Cosmic Circuit: Rajneesh, Sai Baba, Muktananda Gods of the New Age, A lion Paperback*, Chariot Victor Pub, Colorado Spring, 1987.

Flood, Garvin D., *An Introduction to Hinduism (Introduction to Religion)*, Cambridge University Press, New York, 1996.

Gupta, Shakti M., *Vishnu and His Incarnations*, South Asia Books, 1993.

Kasturi, N., *The Life of Bhagavan Sri Sathya Sai Baba (Series on the Life of Sathya Sai Baba)*, Sathya Sai Book Center of America, Tustin, CA, 1989.

Kasturi, N., *Sathyam Shivam Sundaram: The Life of Bhagavan Sri Sathya Sai Baba. Sri Sathya Sai* Educational and Publication Foundation, Withefield. 4 volumes, 1977.

Mason, Peggy and Ron Laing, *Sai Baba: the Embodiment of Love*, Gateway Books, Bath, U.K., 1996.

Murphet, Howard, *Sai Baba: Man of Miracles*, Samuel Weiser, Inc., York Beach, Maine, 1987.

Oxtoby, Willard G., *World Religions: Eastern Traditions*, Second edition, Oxford University Press, New York, 2002.

Roberts, Paul William, *Empire of the Soul: Some Journeys in India*, Riverhead Books, New York, 1994.

Sandweiss, Samuel H., *Sai Baba: The Holy Man and the Psychiatrist*, Birth Day Publishing Company, San Diego, CA, 1975.

Schulman, Arnold *Baba*, The Viking Press, New York, 1971.

Steel, Brian, *The Sathya Sai Baba Compendium: A Guide to the First Seventy Years*, Samuel Weiser, Inc. York Beach, Maine, 1997.

Warner, Judy, *Transformation of the Heart: Stories by Devotees of Sathya Sai Baba*, Red Wheel/Weiser, Boston, MA, 1995.

Wood, Michael, *Legacy: A Search for the Origins of Civilizations*, Network Books, 1992.

FURTHER READING

Babb, Lawrence and Susan Wadley, *Media and the Transformation of Religion in South Asia*, University of Pennsylvania Press, Philadelphia, 1995.

Bassul, Daniel E., *The Incarnation in Hinduism and Christianity: The Myth of the God-Man (Library of Philosophy and Religion)*, Humanities Press, 1986.

Brooke, Tal, *Avatar of Night (Special Millennial Edition)*, End Run Publishing; Millennium edition, 1999.

Caruth, Jeannette, *Song of My Life: A journey to the Feet of Sathya Sai Baba*, Leela Press Inc., 1996.

Haraldson, Erlendur and Sathya Sai Baba, *Modern Miracles: An Investigative Report on Psychic Phenomena Associated with Sathya Sai Baba*, Random House Publishing Group, New York, 1987.

Hislop, Jon S., *Conversations With Sathya Sai Baba*, Birth Day Publishing Company, Bangalore, 1979.

Kumar, Vijaya, *108 Names of Shirdi Sai Baba*, Sterling Publishers Private, Limited, New Delhi, India, 1997.

Murphet, Howard, *Walking the Path with Sai Baba*, Red Wheel/Weiser, Boston, MA, 1993.

Svensson, C., editor, *Bhagavad Gita, with Comments from the Writings of Sathya Sai Baba*, Sathya Sai Book Center of America, Tustin, CA, 1992.

Warren, Marianne, *Unraveling the Enigma: Shirdi Sai Baba in the Light of Sufism*, Sterling Publishers Private, New Delhi, India, Limited, 1999.

INDEX

INDEX

meditation, 49
  Sai Baba on, 65–66, 67–68
mental derangement, Sai Baba's new
  identity as, 30–32
milk-rice, 16, 28
miracles, Sai Baba performing, 3, 17,
  41, 87–88
  and cure of diseased, 3, 9–10, 34,
    43–44, 51–52, 95–103
  and materializing objects, 3,
    16–17, 28, 30, 31, 32, 33, 38, 40,
    86, 88, 97
Murphet, Howard, 40, 41
museums, Sai Baba establishing, 45,
  74, 87
music, at Sai Baba's birth, 13
Muthyalamma, 23

namah, and reciting 108 Names of
  the Lord, 70
namasmarana, 68
Namavali, Sai Baba on reciting, 70
Narasimha Deva, Sai Baba playing
  role of, 22
natural disasters, Sai Baba assisting
  with, 80
nine, meaning of, 70
Nine-point Code of Conduct, of Sai
  Baba, 62

Old Mandir (old temple), 41–43
OM (Aum), 48
  as greeting, 63–64
  and reciting 108 Names of the
    Lord, 70
  Sai Baba on, 66
108 Names of the Lord (Namavali), 70

Penukonda, Sai Baba's visit to, 30
Pirouz, 9–10, 95–103
plays
  Sai Baba embodying gods in,
    17–20, 22, 32
  of village, 12, 16

Poornachandra Auditorium, 45
poverty. See humanitarian works
praise, Sai Baba on, 65–66
prarabdha, 69
Prasanthi Gram, hospital in, 79
Prasanthi Nilayam, 4–9, 43–46, 57,
  74, 78–79, 85–86, 87
prayer, Sai Baba on, 65–66, 67–68
Prema Sai, 52
Premanand, Basava, 88
pujas, 48, 70–71
puranas, 49
Puttaparthi
  hospital in, 44, 78–79, 86, 86–87
  museums in, 45, 74, 87
  Prasanthi Nilayam in, 4–9, 43–46,
    57, 74, 78–79, 85–86, 87
  Sai Baba attending school in,
    16–17
  Sai Baba born in, 3, 12–14
  Sai Baba's reincarnation in, 28,
    30–36, 38, 39, 41
  schools in, 74, 87

rajas, Sai Baba on, 66
Raju, Easwaramma (mother), 12–13,
  14–16, 23, 25, 26, 27, 28, 33, 36
Raju, Kondama (paternal grandfather),
  12, 16
Raju, Pedda Venkappa (father), 12,
  13, 23, 25, 26, 27, 28, 30, 31, 33,
  36
Raju, Seshama (brother), 23, 24–25,
  30, 33, 34
  Sai Baba's letter to, 104–106
Ram (Rama), 39, 49, 50, 63, 103
Ramakrishna, 4
Ramayana, 12, 49
rehabilitation centers, Sai Baba
  establishing, 80
reincarnation, 6
  and Hinduism, 51
  and Sai Baba's new identity, 28,
    30–34, 38, 39, 41, 51–53

INDEX

ABOUT THE CONTRIBUTORS

MASOUD KHEIRABADI is an Iranian American who immigrated to United States in 1976. For three years, he lived in Texas, where he received an M.S. in Agricultural Mechanization from Texas A & M University. In 1979, he moved to Eugene, Oregon, and studied at the University of Oregon, where he received an M.A. and later Ph.D. in cultural geography. He has taught at University of Oregon, Lewis & Clark College, and Marylhurst University. He is currently teaching for the Humanities and International Studies Program at Portland State University.

Professor Kheirabadi's research interests deal with issues of development in developing countries, with a focus on Middle East and South Asia. He is particularly interested in the relationship between religion, politics, and development. Dr. Kheirabadi has published books and articles on these topics. Among his recent publications are *Iranian Cities: Formation and Development*, *Modern World Nations: Iran*, and *Religions of the World: Islam*.

MARTIN E. MARTY is an ordained minister in the Evangelical Lutheran Church and the Fairfax M. Cone Distinguished Service Professor Emeritus at the University of Chicago Divinity School, where he taught for thirty-five years. Marty has served as president of the American Academy of Religion, the American Society of Church History, and the American Catholic Historical Association, and was also a member of two U.S. presidential commissions. He is currently Senior Regent at St. Olaf College in Northfield, Minnesota. Marty has written more than fifty books, including the three-volume *Modern American Religion* (University of Chicago Press). His book *Righteous Empire* was a recipient of the National Book Award.